TALBOT COUNTY MARYLAND

LAND RECORDS

BOOK TWO: 1676–1691

VOLUMES III, IV AND V

COMPILED BY

R. BERNICE LEONARD

HERITAGE BOOKS
2012

HERITAGE BOOKS
AN IMPRINT OF HERITAGE BOOKS, INC.

Books, CDs, and more—Worldwide

For our listing of thousands of titles see our website
at
www.HeritageBooks.com

Published 2012 by
HERITAGE BOOKS, INC.
Publishing Division
100 Railroad Ave. #104
Westminster, Maryland 21157

First printing by R. Bernice Leonard: 1987
Second printing by Family Line Publications
(with single index): 1992

All rights reserved. No part of this book may be reproduced or
transmitted in any form or by any means, electronic or mechanical,
including photocopying, recording or by any information storage
and retrieval system without written permission from the author,
except for the inclusion of brief quotations in a review.

International Standard Book Numbers
Paperbound: 978-1-58549-220-6
Clothbound: 978-0-7884-9398-0

CONTENTS

ABOUT THE INDEXES

Referrals are to the numbered pages of this book; not
those of the land records shown on the lefthand margins.
Be sure to check the entire page for multiple listings.

THE TALBOT COUNTY LAND RECORDS

These abstracts were made from the deed books
in the Clerk's office, Talbot County Courthouse -
in exact chronological order.

Continuing in much the same fashion as their
predecessors, the Clerks made their entries by
chance thus the reader will occasionally find a
sale recorded before the purchase; conveyance bonds
and Letters of Attorney recorded much later than
the deed with which they should have been included.

During the years encompassed by Volumes Three,
Four and Five - 1676 - 1691 - Talbot County still
extended definitely to Chester River on the north
but the reader will discover a few indentures for
land north of this river. Sassafras River, now
the natural division between Kent and Cecil Counties,
and the Bohemia, a few miles to the north and now
a waterway in Cecil County, are mentioned several
times. Since this area was originally Baltimore
County, the researcher is apt to find the names of
Talbot County settlers in the latter county records.
Cecil County was formed from all that part of Baltimore County on the Eastern Shore in 1674.

The Choptank River was admittedly the eastern
border of Talbot, thus the upper part of Caroline
County including Tuckahoe Neck was within the
bounds of Talbot.

TALBOT COUNTY, MARYLAND LAND RECORDS

VOLUME THREE

page

002 18 June 1676 Stephen Tully, Planter, to William Hackett - 250 acres in Chester River called "Ripley." Wit: John Hawkins, John Brodrib.

003 1 Nov. 1676 John Stanley to William Troth - 400 acres, "Troth's Fortune." Wit: Wm. Taylor, John Whittington.

004 16 Feb. 1676 William Gosling to Lawrence Bennett - 50 acres on the north side Choptank River bought of William Harris. Wit: Thomas Vaughn, Edward Banning.

005 15 June 1676 William Harris, Carpenter and his wife Eliza, to William Gosling, Smith - Half of my tract of 100 acres. Wit: James Murphy, John Beard.

007 19 Sept. 1676 John Walker, Planter, to my daughter Margaret Walker (under 15 years) - gift of a cow calf. Wit: Daniel Walker, William Phillips.

008 10 Oct. 1676 Henry Parker to John Coppin - 50 acres, "Parker's Addition" south side St. Michaels River adjoining Parker's land called "Bite." Wit: Roger Grosse, George Hurlock.

009 15 Aug. 1676 Stephen Tully, Planter, and Jane his wife, to Benjamin Pride, Cooper - 100 acres south side Chester River. Wit: William Jones, Daniel Walker.

011 15 Aug. 1676 Stephen Tully of Chester River to Roger Price, Carpenter - 400 acres on south side Chester River in Hambleton's Branch; adjoining Benjamin Pride - part of the 950 acres laid out for Stephen Tully called "Rigby." Wit: Henry Coursey, Richard Lambe.

013 20 Nov. 1676 Stephen Tully to Richard Kenlish - Power of Attorney. Wit: Henry Coursey, Richard Lambe.

014 15 Aug. 1676 Henry Parker, Gent., to Jonathon Hopkinson, Innholder - 400 acres, "Poplar Ridge," on the eastern branch of Wye River adjoining the land laid out for Elizabeth Brown called "Widdow's Chance." Wit: William Hemsley, Thomas Emerson.

015 19 Feb. 1676 Capt. Philimon LLoyd from William Price and Mary, his wife - 300 acres, "Price's Hill" in Wye River opposite the plantation of Mr. William Coursey. Wit: William Hemsley, James Clayland.

017 ___ Oct. 1676 Henry Parker of Miles River to William Southby of Cecil County, Botewright - 400 acres "Parker's Park" in King's Creek, Choptank River. Wit: Thomas Emerson, William Hemsley.

page
019 20 Feb. 1676 Matthew Mason, Planter, Milly, his wife, and Herbert Craft, to Arthur Emory, Planter - 300 acres "Batchelor's Chance" on Wye River. Wit: William Coursey, Henry Brady, James Coursey.

022 1 Aug. 1676 Roger Grosse to Nathaniel Chance - 100 acres, part of the land laid out for Grosse called "Ashby." Wit: Henry Parker, John Aldridge.

023 14 Aug. 1676 William Berry to Richard Webb - "Redford," adjoining "Hackton," laid out for Nicolas Hackett. Wit: Wm. Hill, Thomas Earle.

025 15 Aug. 1676 Thomas Emerson, Planter, and Katherine his wife, to William Hemsley, Gent. - 300 acres "Whetstone" in Wye River adjoining John Wright and William Snaggs. Wit: Matthew Warde, John Bell.

027 4 Dec. 1667 Walthim Graves to his son Richard Graves - 10,000 lbs. of tobacco to be paid on demand when he is twenty-one. Wit: Thos. Colton.

028 31 Jan. 1676 William Sharp, Planter, known as Mr. William Sharp, son and heir of Peter Sharp, Chirurgeon; and Elizabeth, wife of William Sharp, to John Eason, Planter - 700 acres, "Claborne Island" by the name of "Sharp's Island" - formerly in the tenure of John Bateman, Esq.

030 21 Nov. 1676 William Young, Carpender, to John Green, Planter - Bond in amount of 500 lbs. of tobacco. Wit: Thomas Stevenson, Andrew Price.

031 21 Nov. 1676 William Young, Carpender and Frances his wife, to John Greene, Planter - 200 acres "Carpender's Square" in Wye River. Wit: Thomas Stevenson, Andrew Price.

033 27 Nov. 1676 William Burges of Ann Arundell County, Merchant, to William Coursey - Power of Attorney to acknowledge sale of 300 acres called "Southby" to John and Thomas Lewis of Talbot, made in 1673. Wit: Thomas Taylor, Phill. Lloyd.

034 14 Mar. 1676 John Watkins of Ann Arundell County, Gent., executor of John Grosse, Gent., who was the son and heir of Roger Grosse, to John Davis - 200 acres on Myles River. [John Grosse, A. A. Co. Will p.171 Md. Cal. Wills]

037 5 Jan. 1676 John Fowller, and Sarah his wife, to George Robins - 50 acres "Poplar Point" on Tredhaven River. Wit: Joseph James, Nicholas Barkelett.

038 2 Mar. 1676 John Newman to Thomas Galpin - 50 acres called "Grosely" on the south side St. Michaels River adjoining Roger Grosse. Wit: John Stanley, Henry Parker.

039 18 Mar. 1676 Peter Webb of Cecil County to William Bishop and Robert Palmer - 250 acres in Chester River "Bennington" - adjoining the land of Geo. Read. Wit: George Robins, Matt. Warde, Robert Macklin.

041 1 Feb. 1676 William Smyth, Planter, and Elizabeth his wife, to John Morris of Charles County - assignment of 100 acres on north side Choptank

page
River - part of a patent for 400 acres called "Foxhole." Wit: Robert Collson, Robert Bucombe.

042 9 Dec. 1673 Capt. William Burges of Ridge, Ann Arundell County, Merchant, to Thomas and John Lewis - 350 acres on Chester River - granted to John Boughe, called "Bouaghley" adjoining the land of Robert Macklin. Wit: Robert Burle, Richard Ewen.

046 19 Feb. 1675/6 William Price to Peter Sayer - P/A to convey 300 acres called "Price's Hill." Wit: William Hemsley, James Clayland.

046 Last day February 1676/7 Ann Mitchell, wife of John Mitchell of St. Michaels River, to my children - gift of love and affection - to son John Aldridge, 150 acres in Wye River where I lately lived called "Indian Necke" and cattle; to my daughter Grace Aldridge, 250 acres in Wye River called "Ould Mill" and livestock; to son Benjamin Aldridge 100 acres "Indian Necke" and livestock; to son George Aldridge, 100 acres, part of "Indian Necke;" to daughter Mary Aldridge, 1 cow; to son Thomas Aldridge, 1 cow; to son John Bulpitt, 1 cow. Sons under 18 and daughters under 15. Wit: Thomas Stevenson, John Browne.

048 11 Sept. 1676 Nathaniel Evetts of Kent County to Daniel Walker of Talbot - release of any claims made by me. Wit: Thomas Hynson.

048 10 March 1675 Anthony Dawson of Dorchester, Carpenter, to William Hambridge of Dorchester, Planter - moiety of 400 acres, Tuckahoe Creek in Talbot County, called "Dawson's (illegible)" adjoining the land of Philemon Lloyd and Henry Parker's "Lloyd's Park." Wit: John Seward, Nicolas Brewer.

051 18 June 1676 John Guth, Planter, to William Allen, Planter - "Cottingham" in Michel's River - formerly purchased by William Southbee of Jacob Abraham. Wit: Nathaniel Read, George Palmer.

054 9 Feb. 1676 William Smith and Eliza his wife, to Thomas Vaughn, P/A to deliver patent assigned to John Morris. Wit: Philip Stevenson, John Glover.

054 10 Feb. 1677 Peter Dennis of St. Michael's River, to my daughter Mary Dennis - gift of a cow. Wit: Philip Stevenson, William Hemsley.

055 Thomas Youle to William Smyth, Jr. - bond in amount of 15,000 lbs. of tobacco - "whereas William Smyth late of Talbot by word of mouth on his deathbed - - that his son William Smith (sic), Jr. should have 3 cows with calves or calves by their sides for to be delivered unto his only son William as soon as he shall come unto the age of one and twenty years and also desired that his son William Smith, Jr. should be at his own disposing to vouch and labor for himself as soon as he shall be 18 years of age and not before and that he shall be put to school" - know ye that I, Thomas Youle, having married the relict of William Smith, deceased, do engage myself." Wit: Phil. Stevenson, John Glover, Wm. Younge.

page

056 15 Oct. 1675 Ralph Ellstone to his son, Ralph Ellstone, Jr. - tract called "Ellstone," use of a tract called "Brook Hall" and livestock. Wit: Humphrey Davenport, Richard Royston.

057 13 Nov. 1676 Anthony Tall, executor of William Hambridge, deceased, of Dorchester County, to John Brooke of Dorchester Co. - P/A to receive and acknowledge for 200 acres bargained for by Wm. Hambridge. Wit: John Howard, Nicholas Bremer.

058 27 Nov. 1676 William Burges of Ann Arundell Co., Merchant, to William Coursey - P/A to sell 300 acres called "Broughley" to John and Thomas Lewis. Wit: Thomas Taillor, Phi. Lloyd.

059 19 June 1677 Richard Jones, Planter, to William Tilghman, Gent. - 200 acres on Chester River called "Hinson's Towne" - also 50 acres "Goose Quarter" - granted to Richard Jones and John Singleton. Wit: Matt. Warde, Robert Smith, John Bell. Eliza, wife of Richard Jones.

061 8 June 1677 William Hemsley to John Emerson, Carpenter - 300 acres called "Whetstone" - mentions William Thomas Emerson. Wit: John Stanley, Thomas Collins.

063 1 Nov. 1675 William Fowler of Island Creek, Talbot Co., Planter, to Joseph James, Planter - 200 acres of land patented to Edward Lloyd, Esq. and sold to John Eason. Wit: Humphrey Limbery, John Cockes.

068 20 Aug. 1677 Henry Parker to John Summers, Planter - 300 acres "Kingstone" on King's Creek - adjoining "Parker's Park." Wit: John Brooke, Richard Dudley.

070 15 Aug. 1677 John Broadrib and Sibella, his wife, of Choptank River, Planter, to Henry Mathews, Planter - 250 acres "Larrington" on the south side of Chester River. Wit: Tho. Collins, Richard Sturme.

073 12 Aug. 1677 Roger Price, Carpenter, of Harris'es Creek, Talbot County, and Judith his wife to Vincent Lowe, Gent. - 400 acres on the south side of Chester River adjoining Benjamin Pride, being part of the land of Stephen Tully. Wit: William Coombs, Richard Keene.

075 17 Aug. 1677 John Clymor, Planter, to Daniel Ingerson, Planter - one-half of land called "Grantam" on Wye River. Wit: Philip Stevenson, John Brown, John Wilson.

077 6 Nov. 1677 Thomas Norris, Bricklayer, to John Power - 500 acres on Chester River, called "Macklinborough" - adjoining George Read's land and John Singleton. Wit: Wm. Hambleton, Robert Kemp.

080 12 June 1676 William Harris, Carpenter, to William Goslin, Smith - Bond for 5,600 lbs. of tobacco. Wit: James Murphy, John Beard.

081 18 Aug. 1677 Francis Whitwell of Delaware, Planter, to John Stanley - P/A to convey "Graves' Point" to John Edmondson, Merchant; now in the

page
possession of Richard Bayley. Wit: Edward Peck, William Jones.

082 6 April 1677 Philip Stevenson, Gent. to Edward Stevenson - land bought by
me of William Hart; from me by Edward Stevenson and by Edw. Stevenson to
William Finney. Wit: Wm. Hemsley, John Browne.

082 14 Aug. 1676 Stephen Tully, Gent. and Jane his wife, to William Coursey,
Gent. - 950 acres "Ripley" on the south side Chester River. Wit: Wm.
Dobbyne, Arthur Emory, Thomas Emerson, Ja. Coursey.

084 8 Oct. 1677 William Hemsley and Judith his wife, to Arthur Emory, Jr. -
300 acres called "Point" on south side Chester River. Wit: John Molyne,
Ja. Coursey.

085 17 Sept. 1677 Thomas Hathowd, and Anna his wife, to William Sparks -
50 acres (one-half of 100 acres) on north side of St. Michael's River -
land formerly laid out for Francis Maudlin. Wit: Daniel Walker, John
Wheeler, Robert Edmondson, Ralph Elston, Jr.

087 25 Apr. 1677 Henry Parker to Capt. Philemon Lloyd - 400 acres on St. Michael's River called "Ye Addition." Wit: John Barke, Thomas Allen.

088 15 Oct. 1677 Daniel Walker, Planter, and Alice his wife, to John Lewis -
200 acres on south side Chester River, called "Cheshire" - adjoining the
land of Thomas Hinson, Jr. called "Gray's Inn." Wit: John Gilbert, Elizabeth Gilbert.

089 25 July 1677 Joseph James, Planter, to Richard Moore, Planter - land (no
acreage) in Island Creek, Choptank River - adjoining the land of John
Markes. Wit: Samuel Hatton, Richard Willson.

093 15 Oct. 1677 John Standley, Gent., Attorney of Francis Whitwell of Delaware, to John Edmondson - land called "Graves' Point." Wit: James Benson, James Bowdell.

094 15 Oct. 1677 Nathaniel Cleave, Planter, and Joyce his wife, to John
Michell - 185 acres "Winkleton" on St. Michael's River - adjoining Richard
Carter. Wit: Lawrence Knowles, Thomas Walsh.

097 8 Oct. 1677 William Hemsley, Gent. and Judith his wife, to Arthur Emory,
Jr., son of Ann King, late wife of Arthur Emory, Sr. - "Hemsley" on south
side of Chester River. Wit: John Molyne, Ja. Coursey.

098 15 Jan. 1677 Humphrey Davenport, Docktor of Physick, to Edward Elliott,
House Carpenter - 50 acres called "Beach" on St. Michael's River; 200
acres "Davenport" joining with the said "Beach." Wit: John Stanley, Richard Gould.

101 10 Sept. 1675 Anne Eason, wife of John Eason, Planter, to William Crosse,
Merchant - P/A to acknowledge her consent to the sale of land in Island
Creek to William Sharp. Wit: Samuel Hatton, William Fowler.

page
102   167_ James Clayland, Clerk, to daughter Judith Clayland, aged three years and two months - 1 black cow marked with Michael Cawmon's mark and another with my mark - to remain in my father Hemsley's hands; reverting in case of Judith's death to Penelope Hemsley; then to the youngest of Capt. Hemsley's children. Wit: John Molyne, Thomas Thompson.

102 14 Jan. 1677 John Edmondson to John Paddison of Island Creek - bond of assurance re' sale of a parcel of land called "Moorefield." Mentions John Blower of Island Creek. Wit: John Price, Wm. Wintersaill.

103 19 Nov. 1677 John Edmondson, Merchant, and Sarah his wife, to Richard Bailey of Talbot, Gent. - 100 acres on north side Choptank River in Tredhaven Creek, called "Graves." Adjoining the land laid out for William Turner. Wit: William Hemsley, Thomas Vaughan.

105 1 Nov. 1677 John Ashcome of Calvert County to Charles Gorsuch of Baltimore County - 100 acres of land on Dividing Creek, Talbot County - bought of James Edward, Merchant, of Bristol in 1673, adjoining the land laid out for Edward Lloyd. Also 100 acres, "Edmond's Lower Cove, " adjoining the land now in possession of John Ashcombe called "Edmond's Cove;" also 100 acres "Edward's Purchase" adjoining "Edmond's Lower Cove." Wit: Henry Hooper, William Taphill.

107 17 Nov. 1677 John Boone to Geroge Robins - P/A. Wit: Joseph James, Wm. Cadman.

108 17 Dec. 1677 John Boone, Planter, to William Rich - 700 acres "Taylor's Ridge" at the head of St. Miles Creek. Wit: Humphrey Limbury, Joseph James.

110 19 Nov. 1677 William Hemsley, Gent. and Judith his wife, to Ralph Dawson, Cooper - 400 acres on Chester River called "Anthony." Wit: Hugh Sherwood, William Finney.

113 12 Feb. 1677 William Crump and Frances his wife, to Henry Greene - 200 acres "Costain's Hope" on Corsica Creek - adjoining land laid out for Robert Hatton. Wit: Robert Smith, Tho. Bruff.

114 28 Feb. 1677 Eliza Sharpe, wife of William Sharpe, to my brother William Stevens - P/A to convey my interest in 600 acres called "Chestnut Bay" in Tuckahoe Creek to Joseph Padly of Benowby, Kingdon of England. Wit: Hugh Huching, Jone Jones.

115 27 Feb. 1677 Robert Smith to Christopher Denny - 100 acres "Smith's Lott" on the south side Corsica Creek adjoining the land laid out for Nathaniel Evitt. (No witnesses)

118 2 Feb. 1677 William Sharpe and Eliza his wife, to Joseph Padly, Merchant - 600 acres "Chestnut Bay." Wit: Hugh Huching, Jone Jones.

119 15 Oct. 1677 John Davis and Frances his wife, to Winlock Christison - 60 acres in St. Michael's River adjoining land laid out for Roger Grosse, Sr. Wit: Henry Parker, John Michell.

page
122 26 Feb. 1677 Samuel Winslow of Boston Colony in New England, to John
     Broadrib of Talbot - 600 acres on Chester River called "Tattonham."
     Wit: Henry Parker, Roger Gross.

124 15 Feb. 1677 Vincent Lowe, Esq. and Elizabeth his wife, to Richard Gould -
     300 acres on the south side Chester River adjoining the land of Benjamin
     Pride - being part of 950 acres called "Ripley" laid out for Stephen Tully.
     Wit: John Hawkins, Peter Hadaway.

127 12 Feb. 1677 William Crump, Planter, to Henry Greene - Bond. Wit:
     Robert Smith, Thos. Bruff.

128 (no date)   John Boone, Planter, to William Rich - Bond. Wit: Humphrey
     Limbury, Joseph James.

128 25 July 1670 Joseph James of Island Creek, Talbot County, Planter, to
     Richard Moore of H_?_ ding Creek - (The rest of this deed is missing)

129 20 April 1678 John Hollingsworth, Planter, from Ralph Dawson, Cooper, and
     Mabell his wife - 200 acres bought of William Hemsley on Chester River.
     Wit: William Hemsley, Thomas Mountford.

131 10 Mar. 1678 Ralph Dawson, Cooper, and Mabell his wife, to Robert Kemp -
     100 acres on Harris Creek called "Mabell." Wit: Thomas Mountfort, John
     Newman.

134 29 April 1675 Thomas Emerson and Catherine his wife, to Edward Stevenson -
     "Purchase" on the north side of St. Michael's River, east side of Norwich
     Island in Wye River, adjoining Wm. Hemsley's 500 acres purchased from Thos.
     Emerson. Wit: Phillip Stevenson, Roger Gross. A bond was witnessed by
     Richard Dudley and Benjamin Furby.

136 15 Jan. 1678 Thomas Galpin to Henry Parker - 50 acres on south side of
     St. Michael's River called "Norman's Fields" - adjoining the land of Roger
     Gross called "Ashby." Wit: Robert Gouldesburgh, Geo. Robins.

137 Last day of April, 1678 Robert Jenkins of Bullenbrook, Talbot County, Plan-
     ter, to Richard White - 80 acres in Bullenbrook Creek between the plantat-
     ions of Edward Roaper amd the said Richard White - with all appurtenances
     as first granted to John Davis. Wit: Samuell Abbott, Rowland Robson.

141 8 Feb. 1678 John Broadrib to Richard Collins - one-half part of a tract
     granted to Samuel Winslow late of this Province called "Tattenham," con-
     taining 600 acres - which half part if to be the upper half of 300 acres;
     the lower part where John Broadrib is now seated; also one-half of "At-
     well" granted to ye said John Broadrib, in Island Creek in Chester River.
     Wit: Henry Parker, Robert Smith.

144 10 Sept. 1678 John Broadrib to Humphrey Davenport, Chirurgion - 500 acres
     on the north side Chester River called "Biark." Wit: Richard Royston,
     Robert Smith. Broadrib notes "with consent of my wife" - not identified.

page
147   29 April 1678 Lewis Closier, Cooper, and Susannah his wife, to Thomas
      Anderson, Chirurgion - 100 acres, "Jordan's Hill" on Jordan's Creek in
      Choptank River. Wit: John Glover, Robert Knape.

150   27 Sept. 1677 John Boone to George Robins - P/A to acknowledge sale of
      "Taylor's Ridge" - 350 acres on the north side of Choptank River at the
      head of St. Michael's Creek - as appears by indenture from me to William
      Rich. Wit: Joseph James, William Cadman.

151   20 Nov. 1677 Thomas Robins of Talbot to George Robins of Talbot - refers
      to a conveyance between them made in Sept. 1671 as Thomas Robins of Parish
      of St. Mary's See, Bow: London, Mercer and George Robins of Buckingham,
      County of Bucks, Gent. - Thomas assigns one-half of 1000 acres called
      "Job's Content" on the eastern branch of Tredhaven Creek, granted to Job
      Nutt - whereon both Thomas and George are residing. Thomas retains a
      right to egress to the water from his part. Wit: Thomas Martin, John
      Robins, Robt. Gouldsburgh, William Crosse.

164   29 Sept. 1677 William Coursey, Philemon Lloyd, Edward Man and William
      Crosse, Merchants - to Thomas and George Robins - arbitration (division)
      of "Job's Content."

173   26 may 1678 Walter Quinton, Carpenter, to John Morley and John King -
      100 acres "Hack Hill" between the Choptank River and Tredaven Creek.
      Wit: John Stanley, John Ward.

177   20 Aug. 1678 John Pitt of Talbot to Matthew Pitt of Waymouth, County
      Lanchester, England, Merchant - 500 acres called "Vineyard" on the east
      side Tuckahoe Creek adjoining the land of William Jones called "Bristoll"
      and adjoining the land laid out for Nicholas Hackett. Wit: John Baynard,
      John Glover.

181   14 Sept. 1678 Peter Sydes of Wye River, Planter, to William Young -
      part of "Triangle" in Wye River - formerly purchased of Wm. Young.
      Wit: John Stephens, Franciscus Ferdinandus Goyer.

183   16 June 1678 Robert Lambden, Planter, to George Collison, Planter -
      50 acres on the west side of Harris Creek called "Rehobeth." Wit:
      Robert Whaill, Margaret Gasgill.

186   1 June 1678 Samuel White to Silvester Abbott, Jr. (a minor) - White
      married the widow of Silvester Abbott, Sr. who died and left one child,
      Silvester, Jr. Samuel White binds himself to take care of the child and
      give him 1 ould cow, 1 heifer and increase until young Abbott is of age,
      excluding bull calves; also 1 mare colt and the second colt that falls
      and it's increase; also 2 sows and their increase, three years before he
      comes to twenty-one. Wit: Samuel Abbott, Robert Mynott.

187   15 Aug. 1678 John Broadrib and Sibella his wife, to John Salsbury - 100
      acres called "Bradford" on south side Chester River. Wit: John Cawman,
      John Hix.

page
191 28 May 1678 John Stephens, boatwright, of Dorchester County, to John
     Marke of Talbot - "Stephen's Field" on the east side of Tuckahoe Creek,
     containing 1000 acres. Wit: Tho. Gilbert, John Edmundson, John Hooker.

195 29 April 1678 Roger Gross to Charles Bardon - part of 800 acres called
     "Ashby" in St. Michael's River, formerly owned by Roger Gross, Sr. of
     Ann Arundel County - adjoining the land in possession of Nathaniel Cleane.
     Wit: Henry Parker, George Hurlock.

199 18 July 1678 Thomas Mountford, Merchant, to Thomas Vaughan, Gent. -
     200 acres "Hoggshole" and 200 acres "Studd's Point" on the north side of
     Choptank River - formerly taken up by Thomas Manning and Thomas Studs
     and sold to Mountfort - adjoining land laid out for Andrew Skinner and
     Barth Glovin. Wit: Thomas Smithson, James Sedgwick.

204 18 Apr. 1678 Ralph Dawson and Mable his wife, to David Fairbank, Plan-
     ter - 50 acres on the western side of Second Creek called "Upp Holland."
     Wit: Thomas Mountford, John Power.

209 17 Sept. 1678 John Miller registers his cattle mark and a Bill of Sale.

209 20 Aug. 1678 Christopher Parke, Schoolmaster, and Priscilla, his wife,
     to Nicholas Hackett, Planter - consignment of a Bill of Sale. Wit:
     Stephen Joardan, Walter Quinton.

210 15 August 1678 John Broadrib and Sibella his wife, to Matthew Brown -
     500 acres "Stoke" on the south side of Chester River adjoining the land
     laid out for Samuel Winslow, now in possession of John Broadrib. Wit:
     Thomas Cawman, John Hix.

214 10 Oct. 1678 William Kirkum, Planter, and Alice his wife, to Henry
     Bowen, Planter - 300 acres "Mt. Snowden" on the north side Choptank
     River. Wit: R. Turner, John Stanley.

218 20 Aug. 1678 William Kirkum to John Stanley - P/A. Wit: John Hatton,
     John Ward.

219 20 Aug. 1678 John Edmondson, Attorney for Robert Curtis of Virginia,
     Planter, to John Paddison, Planter - "Moorefield Addition" adjoining the
     land laid out for Francis Parrott called "Rich Range" and John Anderton -
     adjoining the land of Thomas Eston - and also a parcel adjoining next to
     the land of Andrew Skinner, "Fostall" - 250 acres. (no witnesses)

222 17 Sept. 1678 John James and Thomas Roe, Planters, to Cowley and Ann
     his wife - mort. - 137 acres in Wye River - formerly in the tenure of
     John Slater, deceased. Wit: William Combes, Samuel Hatton.

228 16 Sept. 1678 George Cowley, Gent., and Anne his wife to John James
     and Thomas Roe - 137 acres "Hambleton's Park" in Wye River. Wit: Wm.
     Cross, William Combes, Samuell Hatton.

233 19 Nov. 1678 George Cowley and Ann his wife, to Richard Richardson

page

and John Preston - 600 acres at the head of St. Michael's Creek called "Hatton" - adjoining the land laid out for Andrew Skinner and Francis Digges called "Frankland St. Michaels" - the same laid out by William Hemsley 1 Sept. 1673 for Samuel Hatton, his wife Eliza and George Cowley, jointly. Wit: Thomas Alexander, John Marke, William Crosse.

236   12 Nov. 1678 William Hemsley, Gent., to John Whittington of Kent County, Planter - 500 acres on east side of Chester River called "Hemsley's Britland" - adjoining land laid out for John and William Coursey called "Coursey Towne." Wit: Hugh Sherwood, George Barber.

239   17 Dec. 1678 John Boone, Planter, to George Robins - P/A to sell 350 acres at head of St. Michael's Creek called "Taylor's Ridge" to William Rich. Wit: Joseph James, William Cawman.

240   18 Oct. 1678 Henry Willcocks to Michael Hackett, Planter - 300 acres in Chester River called "Mt. Hope" - mention John Rawlings. Wit: William Montique, John James.

241   18 Nov. 1678 Michael Hackett to Henry Willcocks - Mortgage. Wit: Samuel Hatton, Richard Moore.

244   23 Sept. 1678 Samuel Hatton and Eliza his wife to George Cowley - release of 600 acres of land. Wit: Wm. Crosse, Thomas Camm, John Eyres.

249   12 Nov. 1678 William Hemsley and Judith his wife to John Whittington - Bond. Wit: Hugh Sherwood, George Barber. Judith Hemsley's acknowledgment witnessed by Will. Gary, George Barber.

250   12 Sept. 1678 William Porter and Ann his wife to the four sons of Thomas Camper, deceased, Thomas, Robert, William and John - gift of cattle and one to be taken out for my daughter Ann at her day of marriage. Wit: Alexander Larrimore, Roger Price.

250   18 Nov. 1678 Michael Hackett, Planter, to John Burrows, Planter - 100 acres in Island Creek, part of a tract belonging to Henry Willcockes called "Mt. Hope" - now sold to Michael Hackett. Wit: William Hackett, Roger Robberts.

251   18 Nov. 1678 Michael Hackett, Planter, to John Burrows - 100 acres, formerly Henry Willcockes' called "Mt. Hope." Wit: William Hackett, Roger Roberts.

255   16 Dec. 1678 William Wattson of Dorchester County, Planter, to Robert White of Talbot - 150 acres in Harris Creek, north side Cuthbert's Cove. Wit: Roger Price, William Jump.

257   2 Dec. 1678 Robert Smith, Gent., to Thomas Jones, Planter - 300 acres on the south side of Chester River adjoining land laid out for Richard Tilghman, called "Bartholomew's Plaine." Wit: James Sedgwick, Henry Price, Ja. Coursey.

page
261   1678 The petition of Thomas Harvie for freedom - indentured to
       Robert Everidge and sold to Bryan Omealy for a term of four years. Ordered
       to be freed. Wit: Joseph Billiter.

262 10 June 1678 Nicholas Hackett and Mary his wife, Planter, to Joseph Bil-
     liter, Plasterer - 600 acres called "Hackett's Garden" on east side Tucka-
     hoe Creek. Wit: Thomas Anderson, George Hurlocke.

264 19 day 9ber 1678 Robert Harding and Rachell his wife to Bryan Omealy -
     250 acres "Batchelor's Range" at the head of St. Michael's River.

265 18 day, 12th month called Feb. 1678 Henry Parker, Planter, to James Bar-
     ber, Planter - part of land called "Holden's Addition" on Fausley Branch -
     adjoining the land of Roger Gross. Wit: Wm. Tilghman, James Scott.

267 16 Dec. 1678 Thomas Vaughn, Gent., to Robert Pearson, Planter - 100 acres
     called "Contention" in Second Creek - adjoining the land of the widow Mar-
     tin. Wit: Ja. Coursey, Willm. Hemsley.

269 20 Jan. 1678 Henry Parker, Gent., to Thomas Smithson, Merchant - "Holden's
     Addition" south side Fausley Branch, "Holden" 225 acres; also 50 acres,
     "Bite;" also 200 acres "Mill Road." Wit: George Robins, James Eustis,
     James Coursey.

275 9 Jan. 1678 Thomas Vaughn, Gent., to William Trayman - 400 acres of land;
     200 acres laid out for Thomas Studd called "Studd's Point;" 200 acres laid
     out for Thomas Manning called "Hoggshole." Wit: Ja. Coursey, Wm. Hemsley.

278 14 Nov. 1678 Robert Hawkshaw, Pltr., to John Hollingsworth, Planter -
     50 acres, "Collin's Lott" in Chester River adjoining the land of Alexander
     Maxwell - part of 300 acres laid out for Thomas Collins, ourchased by Jo-
     seph Dellawood and sold to Thomas Mayrick, partner with Robert Hawkshaw.
     Wit: Richard Jaxson, John Gilbert.

281 28 Feb. 1677 Col. Vincent Lowe to Charles Hollingsworth - 300 acres on the
     south side of Chester River called "Brimington." (no witnesses).

283 5 Jan. 1678 John Duncombe of Talbot (late of Virginia), Planter, to Wm.
     Combes, Merchant and Eliza his wife, daughter and heir of Edward Roe -
     land in Island Creek, devised to Thomas Duncombe, Jr., one of the sons of
     Mary, late wife of Edward Roe; and a minor brother to John Duncombe, the
     said Thomas, Jr. died under age twenty-one. The plantation now in tenure
     of Francis Harrison under a lease made by Edward Roe. Wit: Wm. Crosse,
     Joshua Atkins, William Warner. [Edward Roe died 1676, devised "Batchelor's
     Plantation" in Island Creek to Thomas 'Duncan.'][Md. Cal. Wills Vol. I:173]

285 13 Mar. 1678 John Clymer, Planter, to Daniel Ingerson and Henry Snoden,
     Planters - 200 acres called "Grantham" - adjoining land laid out for Thom-
     as Williams near head of Wye River. Wit: Wm. Hemsley, Phillip Stevenson.

287 4 March 1678/9 John Newman, Planter, to Robert Hillton, Physician -
     Assignment of a deed of sale. Wit: Richard Astin, Richard Parnes, John
     Gilbert.

page

288 3 March 1678 William Hackett and Katherine his wife, Planter, to Peter Haddaway, Planter - 100 acres - part of 200 acres sold to Hackett by Stephen Tully, called "Ripley" - adjoining the land of Richard Gould, south side Chester River. Wit: Robert Smith, John Whittington.

293 Last day of January 1678 John Edmondson to John Stanley during his natural life - part of a tract called "North Yorke" near the grounds formerly seated by Roger Somers. Wit: Robert Jenkinson, Thomas Brown, Henry Parker.

295 8 Nov. 1678 Stephen Tully, Gent., and Jane his wife, to Robert Ellis, Plasterer - 400 acres, part of "Providence" on south side Chester River - laid out for Andrew Skinner, Samuel Winslow and Henry Parker and by them divided; this 400 acres intended to be conveyed to John Underwood, now deceased wherein James Monke did dwell - mentions John Scott as a late tenant. Wit: James Sedgwick, Ja. Coursey.

298 __ Jan. 1678 Robert Harding, with consent of Rachel his wife, to Bryan Omealy, Planter - tract called "Bachelor's Range" between Miles River and King's Creek branches. Wit: Jacob Abraham, Will. Lupton.

299 17 June 1679 John Edmondson and Sarah his wife, to Francis Neale, Planter - 150 acres called "Cuba," between two branches at the head of "Edmondson's Freshes," now in occupation of Robert Brian - adjoining "Lower Dover." Wit: Emanuel Jenkinson, Edward Hargreaves.

301 15 Aug. 1679 Robert Noble and Cornelia, his wife, to Michael Russell - part of "Tilghman's Fortune" and part of "Cornelias's Coole Spring" lying in Treadhaven Creek - against the house now in the possession of John Pitt - containing 106 acres. Wit: George Parrott, John Baynard.

302 19 Aug. 1679 John Nunam to Obadiah Judkin - 50 acres, "Nunam" - head of the eastern branch of St. Michael's River adjoining the land formerly laid out for William and John Shaw called "Cottingham" and land laid out for John Jadwin. Wit: John Banister, Thomas Breerley, Henry Parker.

304 12 Aug. 1679 Edward Stevens (Stevenson), Planter, to Robert Noble and Simon Stevens (Stevenson), Planters - one-half of 200 acres "Planter's Delight" in Wye River. Wit: John Baynard, John Chase.

305 _____ 1679 Paule Dorrell of Ann Arundell County, kinsman and heir of Thomas Turner, late of Ann Arundell, Planter, to Thomas Bucknall of Ann Arundell, Planter - 200 acres, "Turner's Ridge," - granted Thomas Turner in 1669 - adjoining land laid out for Thomas Francis. Wit: Wm. Gary, John Bird.

308 18 Aug. 1679 Thomas Bucknall of Ann Arundell County, Sawyer, to John Bird of Broad Neck, Ann Arundell County - "Turner's Ridge," conveyed by Paule Dorrell, the next heir of Thomas Turner. Wit: William Gary, Paule Dorrell.

309 15 Jan. 1678 George Cowley, Gent., and Ann his wife, to Richard Cornich, Merchant - 300 acres called "Sutton" at the head of Michaels Creek,

page
adjoining "Nomany" - commonly called or known by the name of "Capt.
Cowley's Quarter." Wit: William Crosse, William Dickenson, Charles Dickenson.

311 9 Sept. 1679 Henry Matthews and Jane his wife, of Chester, to John Pearle
of Chester - 150 acres called "Larrington" on south side Chester River.
Wit: William Crump, Hugh Johnson.

313 13 Sept. 1679 John Pearle and Elizabeth his wife, Planter, of Chester
River, to William Crump - above. Wit: Nicholas Ponds, Wm. Moffat.

314 9 Sept. 1679 Henry Costin of Wye River, Carpenter, to Sarah and Judith
Wollman, daughters of Richard Wollman - to Judith, 100 acres, Long Tom's
Creek, Wye River, called "Doctor's Gift" - adjoining the land of Richard
Wollman called "The Addition" - to Sarah, 50 acres called "Sarah's Lott"
adjoining the land of Richard Carter now in the possession of Jonas Davis.
Wit: Robert Mynott, Jane Hay.

315 14 Aug. 1679 William Berry to Richard Webb - Conveyance of a bond for
7000 lbs. of tobacco dated 1676. Wit: John Clemans, John Vickery.

315 19 Nov. 1679 Elizabeth Smith, wife of Matthew Smith, former wife of
Christopher Thomas, deceased, to Trustram Thomas, Gent., of Wye River -
quit claim to tract of 350 acres called "Barbadoes Hall" - patented 1665
to Christopher Thomas - on the south side of Chester River. Wit: Wm.
Finney, John Stanley.

316 16 Nov. 1679 John Pitt to William Kircume - 175 acres called "Youghall"
on north side Choptank River adjoining land laid out for John Ingram
called "Tuttlefield." Wit: William Wrench, Jon. Sargeant.

317 17 May 1679 Henry Michell, Planter, of Calvert County, to Edward Turner -
P/A to acknowledge 300 acres "Michell's Hall" in Island Creek, Great Chop-
tank River, to Thomas Bowdle of Calvert County, Planter. Mentions Att-
well's Cove and the land of Attwell Bodwell; also land of Edward Lloyd,
Esq. Wit: Charles Clagett, John Hollins, J. Broome, Wm. Turner.
Peter Wagley, Jane Shipard, Wit. P/A.

318 30 8ber 1679 John Wells and Martha his wife to Peter Sides - 450 acres
at head of Back Wye River. The patent, dated 1 April 1672, from Charles
Calvert to John Wells of Kent, signed by Robert Ridgley, Clerk, recorded.
Wit: William Coursey, Chas. Banckes, Bonham Turner.

319 20 Jan. 1679 Michaell Rogers and Elizabeth his wife, to Robert Parvis,
Taylor - 150 acres called "Highfield" at the head of a small run of
Tuckahoe Creek. Wit: Oliver Millington, Michaell Russell.

321 19 Jan. 1679 Alexander Ray to James Murphy - 150 acres "Raye's Point"
and 100 acres, "The Inlargement" - on north side Choptank River in Second
Creek. Wit: Hugh Sherwood, Patrick Ward.

323 17 Jan. 1679 John Whittington, Planter, to John Barker, Carpenter -
one-half of a parcel of 400 acres called "Lower Dover," 200 acres ad-

page

joining "Dover" - mentions Bill of Sale passed from John Edmondson to John Whittington and John Barker in 1670 and a division between them. Wit: Richard Gurling, John Stanley, Samuel Crayker.

324 17 Jan. 1679 John Barker, Carpenter, to John Whittington, Planter - 200 acres - one-half of "Lower Dover" - adjoining the land of Daniell Jenefer. Wit: R. Gurling, J. Stanley, S. Crayker.

325 10 Mar. 1679/80 Simon Irons, Cooper, to Richard Royston, Gent. - 400 acres on the east side of Broad Creek called "Yafford's Neck." Wit: Thomas Smithson, Andrew Price, Tho. Impey. Dorothy, wife of Simon Irons.

328 22 Feb. 1679 Abraham Sanders, Planter, and Ann his wife, to Edward Kitchener, Planter - 50 acres "Freeman's Rest" - adjoining land taken up by George Prous. Wit: Thos. Smithson, Thos. Mountfort.

329 4 Feb. 1679 Charles Gorsuch of Talbot, Planter, to John Hollins and John Mullikin, P/A. Wit: Samuel Hatton, Richard White.

Charles Gorsuch of Talbot and Sarah his wife, to William Stevens of Island Creek - 300 acres on the east side of Dividing Creek, laid out for James Edwards, Merchant, of Bristol, and purchased of Edwards by John Ashcombe of Calvert County and from Ashcombe by me. Wit: Samuel Abbott, John Groves. Bond given by Gorsuch witnessed by Samuel Hatton and Richard White.

331 16 Mar. 1679/80 Richard Dudley, Taylor, and Elinor, his wife, to Richard Purnell, Planter - 200 acres on the east side of Tuckahoe Creek adjoining the land of John Markes - called "Dudley's Chance." Wit: John Baynard, Thomas Austin.

332 9 Mar. 1679 William Hemsley, Gent., to William Bishopp - a watermill and 10 acres on Corsica Creek - part of a tract of 900 acres in the occupation of John Tillotson. Wit: Stephen Whelewright, Robert Mynott.

334 16 Mar. 1679 Robert Page, Planter, and Hanah his wife, to Humphrey Davenport of Talbot, Cherurgion - 500 acres south side Chester River, in Corsica Creek - called "Welsh Ridge." Wit: Thos. Delehay, Benjamin Randall.

335 15 Mar. 1679 Mary Ward to her brother William Tilghman - P/A. Wit: Jon. Swayne, Robert Macklin.

336 12 Feb. 1679 Mary Ward of Chester River, Widdow, to Richard Swetman of Wye River, Innholder - 650 acres called "Green Spring." Wit: Wm. Tilghman, John Lillingston, Robert Macklin.

338 16 Mar. 1679 John Newnam, Planter, and Jane his wife, to Andrew Orem, Cooper - 300 acres called "Bantry" on the south side of St. Michael's River - adjoining the land laid out for Roger Gross called "Ashby" and "Cottingham," laid out for John and William Shaw. Wit: Thomas Impey, Daniell Walker.

page
340 11 June 1680 William Young, Carpenter, and Frances his wife, to John
     Serjeant, Cooper - 200 acres near the head of Wye River called "Hopewell" -
     adjoining the land of Peter Sides. Wit: William Bonham, Ja. Coursey.

342 25 May 1680 Nicholas Hackett, Planter, and Mary his wife, to Mary Roe,
     widdow, William Combes, Gent. and Elizabeth, his wife - 100 acres on the
     northeast branch of Tredhaven Creek, called "Cardiff" - adjoining land
     laid out for Andrew Skinner called "Piney Point" and land laid out for
     Thomas Taylor - now in the tenure of John Price. Wit: John Rousby, John
     Man.

343 14 June 1680 Henry Parrott, Planter, to William Parrott, Planter - an
     exchange of a tract laid out for Henry Woolchurch called "Middle Spring"
     now in the tenure of Henry Parrott , adjoining his plantation, for a
     part of "Middle Spring" now in the tenure of William Parrott - in Tucka-
     hoe Creek. Wit: John Stanley, James Benson, Griffith Jones.

344 14 June 1680 William Parrott to Henry Parrott - same as above.

346 15 May 1680 Richard Royston to Thomas Impey - P/A. Wit: James Sedgwick,
     Samuel Farmer.

346 15 May 1680 Richard Royston, Gent., to Thomas Loggings, Planter - 300
     acres called "Upper Dover" on north side Choptank River - purchased by
     John Hodges, Sr. from John Richardson, now in the tenure of Thomas Log-
     gings. Wit: Thomas Impey, James Sedgwick.

347 14 June 1680 Henry Costin, Planter, to Thomas Youle, Planter - 200 acres
     called "Lambeth Field" at the head of Wye River adjoining land laid out
     for Thomas Williams. Wit: Jno. Sargeant, Robert Page.

348 15 June 1680 Mary Tilghman, widdow, to John Lillingston - P/A. Wit:
     Simon Wilmer.

349 10 May 1680 Mary Tilghman, widdow, and William Tilghman, her son, to
     Francis Maudlin (Morling) - 500 acres on the south side St. Michael's
     River called "Brantrey" - surveyed for William Smith of St. Mary's Co. -
     adjoining the land of Andrew Skinner called "Spring Close." Wit: John
     Lillingston, Henry Parker.

350 15 June 1680 John Squires of Talbot, Planter, to Robert Evans of Talbot,
     Planter - 50 acres called "Killingsworth" on north side Choptank River
     adjoining the land of Thomas Studd on Bugby Creek. Wit: William Wattson,
     Lewis Nevell.

351 10 June 1680 Robert Smith, Planter, to Thomas Jones, Planter - 300 acres
     on Corsica Creek called "Pleasant Spring." Wit: Jno. Lillingston, Wm.
     Tilghman.

353 15 June 1680 Stephen Tully, Gent., and Jane his wife, to John Hawkins,
     Gent. - "Macklin," 100 acres in Coursey's Creek adjoining the land late
     of James Bowlingsley - also that plantation where Stephen Tully did dwell
     and also "Bowlingsley" adjoining "Macklin," 250 acres; and also a neck

page

of land granted by Henry Coursey, Gent. to John Tully, father of Stephen
Tully. Wit: Michael Turbutt, Ja. Coursey. Bond given by S. Tully was
witnessed by Will. Coursey, Michael Turbutt, and Ja. Coursey.

355 10 Nov. 1679 Walter Kerby of Kent County, Cooper, and Jane his wife, to
Robert Page of Kent, Planter - 500 acres called "Welsh Ridge." Wit:
Charles Banks, Alise Watters.

357 15 June 1680 John Edmondson, Merchant, to Thomas Hutchinson, Tanner -
200 acres called "North Yorke" and another tract adjoining (no name) -
in the freshes of Tredhaven Creek adjoining to "Cook's Mannor," the land
of John Stanley and of John Edmondson. Wit: Thomas Brown, Thomas Dawson.

359 15 June 1680 John Edmondson, Merchant, and Sarah his wife, to John Morris,
of Talbot, Planter - 400 acres in King's Creek called "Adventure" - adjoining land laid out for Joseph Lane. Wit: John Baynard, Robert Evans.

360 15 June 1680 Henry Parrott, Planter, to William Parrott, Planter - bond
for four score pounds sterling. Wit: Jos. Atkinson, Griffith Jones.

361 27 August 1680 Thomas Taylor came into Court and requested a patent to
be recorded dated 1643, for 350 acres of land in Lower Norfolk County
on the Elizabeth River in Virginia. "Francis Wiat, acting under orders
of the Governor and Council to assign land to all adventurers and planters
as have been visual heretofore in like cases either for adventurers of
money or transportation of people to the colony according to the orders of
the late Company and since allowed by his Majestie and likewise that there
be the same proportion of 50 acres granted for every person that hath beene
transported to the colony since midsoomer (sic) 1625 - assigns to Thomas
Marsh alias Rivers 150 acres in the upper county of New Norfolke - when
he or his assigns shall have sufficiently peopled and planted the same -
on Elizabeth River, on the southern branch, called "Oyster Shell Neck" -
granted to Peter Montague 22 Feb. 1637 for transporting 3 persons whose
names are in the patent." Thomas Marsh was given a term of three years
to comply with the terms. Written 21 March 1639.

362 14 Aug. 1680 Lawrence Porter, Planter, to John Price, Bricklayer - part
of "Mt. Misery" in Second Creek - patented by Thomas Hethod and from him
purchased by James Murphy and from Murphy by William Bell and from Bell
by Lawrence Porter.. Wit: Hugh Sherwood, Griffith Jones.

364 20 Nov. 1679 Robert Smith of Chester River, Planter, to William Hatfield
and John Barwick of Wye River, Planters - 800 acres "Normanton." Wit:
Richard Jones, Thomas Emerson.

365 12 Mar. 1680 Nicholas Hackett, Planter, and Mary his wife, to Thomas Anderson, Chirurgion - 300 acres "Hackett's Garden," on east side Tuckahoe
Creek. Wit: John Price, Robert Poure.

366 16 Mar. 1679/80 John Richardson of Dorset County to John Edmondson - P/A.
Wit: John Morley, John Stanley.

17.

366 12 Aug. 1680 John Richardson of St. Jones, Province of New York, to Edward Pond of Talbot - 250 acres on the eastern branch of Tredhaven Creek
called "Jamaica" - adjoining the land of Mr. Jennings. Wit: John Edmondson, John Alford.

367 14 Aug. 1680 George Robins, Gent., and Margaret his wife, to Walter Quinton - 400 acres called "Goldsborough" at the head of Tredhaven Creek - only
150 acres hereby conveyed. Wit: Thomas Impey, Edward Lydenham. Robins'
bond was witnessed by Thomas Browne and Robert Goldsborough.

369 18 Oct. 1680 Mary Ward, widdow, to James Coursey - P/A. Wit: Simon Wilmer, Charles Hinson.

369 18 Oct. 1680 Mary Ward, widdow, to William Tilghman and John Lillingston -
to ensure the maintenance of Matthew Tilghman Ward, her son and the orphan
son of Matthew Ward, her late husband - conveys plantation "Winton," 500
acres, south side Chester River; "Winton's Addition," 25 acres; also another 50 acres called "Winton's Addition;" also a tract called "Adventure;"
1000 acres in Talbot County on the south side of Chester River at the head
of Double Creek, patented 6 June 1673; also "Ward Oake," 400 acres on the
north side of Chester River, patented 1 June 1673; all to be received by
Matthew Tilghman Ward when he is 21. Also he is to receive four negro servants and in case soe many cannot be purchased, then eight English men servants and in case they cannot be procured then the full value of either the
negroes or servants is to be paid when he is 21. Lillingston and Tilghman
to purchase 7 cows with calves and 1 bull to be delivered when he arrives
to 21. Wit: Elias King, Simon Wilmer.

371 18 Oct. 1680 William Young, Planter, and Frances his wife, to Nehemish
Covington of Talbot, Planter - in consideration of two men servants; 2400
lbs. of tobacco and also 3600 lbs. of tobacco - the dwelling and plantation whereon Covington resides near the head of Wye River; also part of a
tract of 450 acres now in three parts divided, called "Young's Chance,"
granted to John Grey and William Young; also a tract called "Triangle,"
125 acres, granted in 1664 to Andrew Skinner and purchased by Young from
Peter Sides - in all 185 acres. Wit: Tho. Emerson, Andrew Price.

374 16 Nov. 1680 Michael Hackett, Planter, to Henry Willcocks - 100 acres of
land in Island Creek - part of a tract of 300 acres called "Mt. Hope" -
adjoining land sold by Hackett to John Barrowes and adjoining Henry Will-
cock's now dwelling. Charles Hollingsworth, Attorney for Willcocks.
Wit: John Pearle, William Crafford.

TALBOT COUNTY, MARYLAND LAND RECORDS

VOLUME FOUR

page
001 18 Jan. 1680 John Nunam, Planter, and Jane his wife, to Dennis Hopkins, Planter - "Coventry" - in King's Creek. Wit: Thos. Impey, Wm. Jump.

003 18 Jan. 1680 William Gibson, Planter, and Ann his wife, to Thomas Hopkins, Planter - 250 acres called "Maxwell Moore" - on western branch of Tredhaven Creek. Wit: Robert Towe, John Kelly.

003 18 Jan. 1680 Miles Gibson of Baltimore and Ann his wife, to Samuel Hatton and John Holland - P/A. Wit: Fra. Lovelace, Lewis Barton.

005 25 May 1680 Miles Gibson of Baltimore County and Ann his wife, to Wm. Troth - 300 acres called "Cole Banks" - on the northeast branch of the Choptank River adjoining the land laid out for William Moore - having twice fallen into the hands of Thomas Thursten - and now in the tenure of Miles Gibson. Wit: Fra. Lovelace, Jane Page.

006 Miles Gibson and Charles Gorsuch to William Troth - bond for 8000 lbs. of tobacco. Wit: Fra. Lovelace, Jane Page.

007 18 Jan. 1680 Michael Hackett, Planter, and Mary his wife, to John Persons - 50 acres in Island Creek, south side Chester River, called "High Gate" - adjoining the lands of John Hawkins, John Singleton and Thomas Norris. Wit: Henry Willcocks, Peter Wilson.

008 18 Jan. 1680 John Persons, Planter, and Damerous his wife, to Peter Willson of Cecil County - 200 acres in Chester River on the southeast branch called "Spread Eagle" - begins at a poplar, the uppermost bounded tree of 1000 acres taken up for Daniel Jenefer, now of Accomack and since sold to John Parsons and Damarus his wife. Wit: Henry Willcocks, Michael Hackett.

010 19 Dec. 1680 John Hammond of Ann Arundell Co. to William Parot of Talbot - P/A witnessed by John Baynard, Samuell Farmer.

010 4th day, 8th month, 1680 John Hammond of Ann Arundell Co. to John Judgwin of Talbot, Planter - 550 acres on Tuckahoe Creek called "Hampton" - adjoining land laid out for Thomas Turner called "Harley Field." Wit: J. Hillen, John Wotters, John Hammond.

011 14 Mar. 1680 John Michell, Planter, to Michaell Hackett - 200 acres in Chester River called "Josseland.' Mention Henry Willcockes and John Hawkins. Wit: Michael Miller, Timothy Mounsier.

013 14 Mar. 1680 Thomas Smithson to John Coppin - 12 acres, part of a tract called "Bight" on St. Michael's River - adjoining the dwelling plantation of John Coppin and a tract called "Tilghman's Fortune." Wit: William Chance, Thomas Booker.

page
014 10 mar. 1680 George Robins, Gent., to John Squires, Planter - 150 acres, part of tract "Goldesborough" on Tredhaven Creek. With consent of Margaret Robins, his wife. Wit: Thos. Robins, John Robins, Robert Goldesburgh.

015 8 Nov. 1677 Hugh Magregor of Cecill Co. to Walter Kerby of Kent, Cooper - 500 acres on Corsica Creek called "Welsh Ridge." Wit: Anthony Workman, Edward Cox.

017 15 Mar. 1680/81 Michael Hackett and Mary his wife to Timothy Mount-sier - 150 acres, "Hackett's Delight" - in Chester River. Wit: Robert Appletree, Thomas Lewis.

018 _____ 1681 Capt. Humphrey Davenport to his beloved daughter, Kather-ine Wells - moiety of "Welsh Ridge" in Chester River - containing in all 500 acres. Wit: James Murphy, James Downes.

019 21 June 1681 Simon Irons of St. Jones in New York province, Carpenter, to Richard Sweatman of Wye River, Innholder - 600 acres in Chester Riv-er - one moiety of "Royston" - purchased of Richard Royston. Wit: Wm. Hemsley, Thos. Impey.

021 20 June 1681 Abraham Hurlock to John Stuart - 50 acres, "Abraham's Chance" - north side Choptank River, at the head of the northeast branch of Tredhaven Creek - adjoining "Abraham's Lott" and the lands of Wm. Sharp. Wit: Henry Parker, Daniell Walker.

022 25 Feb. 1681 William Colborne of Somerset, Gent., and Margaret his wife, to Griffith Jones one of the attorneys of Talbot County - P/A to convey to Richard Hall of Talbot, part of "Smith's Clifts" - and to John Wotters of Talbot - 400 acres of "Smith's Clifts." Hall obtained 560 acres of the same - adjoining the land of Peter Sharp and John Homewood. Wit: George Cowley, Griffith Jones.

026 15 Mar. 1681 Stephen Tully, Planter, to John Tilleson and Thomas Bing-am of Talbot, Planters - 300 acres, "Lord's Gift" in Corsica Creek. Adjoining "Upper Deale." Wit: Robert Ellis, Edward Barraclift.

027 16 June 1681 Stephen Tully, Planter, to Robert Moulder and John Beech-er, Planters - 300 acres in Corsica Creek called "Tully's Reserve." Wit: Tho. Bruff, James Eustis.

028 21 June 1681 Edward Pond, Planter, and Ann his wife, to Humphrey Davis, Cordwinder - 200 acres in Tredhaven Creek adjoining the land of Mr. Jennings - "Jamaica," patented 1676. Wit: Thos. Anderson, Tho. Delehay.

030 15 Mar. 1681 John Hollingsworth and Jane his wife, to Thomas Carman - 50 acres in Chester River called "Collington" - formerly belonging to Alexander Maxfield. Wit: Josias Wainewright, Jonas Greenwood.

033 13 June 1681 Peter Hathaway, Carpenter, to William Hackett, Planter - 100 acres south side Chester River called "Ripley" - formerly Stephen Tully's. Wit: J. Whittington, Richard Gould.

page

036 3 Mar. 1681 John Breame, Planter, and Mary his wife, to Thomas Wether-by, Carpenter - 300 acres, "Ashton" - Hambleton's Creek in Chester River. Wit: William Hackett, Jonas Greenwood.

038 4 June 1681 Stephen Tully, Planter, to John Breame, Planter - 300 acres in Chester River called "Ashton." Wit: Thos. Carman, Thomas Wetherby.

040 10 June 1681 Sebilla Broadrib, widdow of John Broadrib of Talbot, to Samuel Randall, Planter - 250 acres on Island Creek, south side Chester River - one moiety or one-half of "Freshford." Wit: Benjamin Randall, Christopher Goodhand, Ja. Coursey.

042 21 June 1681 Henry Pratt and Seath his wife, to Edward Baracliffe of Talbot - 50 acres, part of "Wilton." Wit: Robert Smith, Daniel Ingerson.

043 20 June 1681 Sarah Eastgate, wife of Caleb Eastgate, lately known by the name of Sarah Elingsworth late wife of William Elingsworth, to John Stanley - 400 acres called "Salsberry Plaine" in Tuckahoe Creek - adjoining the land laid out for John Edmondson and adjoining land laid out for Capt. Philemon Lloyd - patented to John Richardson in 1673; sold to Edward Williams, 1673; sold to Robert Turner, 1673; and given to the several children of William Elingsworth born of the body of the said Sarah Elingsworth. Wit: Richard Bayly, Thos. Hutchinson.

046 10 June 1681 John Hawkins, Gent., and Frances his wife, to Hon. Vincent Lowe - P/A - "Whereas John Grose of Ann Arundel by his last will and testament dated 4 December 1675 did devise to Frances, now wife of John Hawkins by name of Frances Grose, 250 acres in Miles River, Talbot Co., on Fausley Branch, called "Fausley" - Hawkins and Lowe convey to Michael Turbutt and Sarah his wife for the term of her (Sarah's) natural life and afterwards to her heirs. Wit: Richard Peacocke, George Robins, Ja. Coursey.

049 ___ Sept. 1681 Daniel Jenifer and Ann his wife of Accomack Co., Va., to William Hemsley, Gent. of Talbot - P/A in Talbot County Court to acknowledge two deeds: one to John Parsons conveying 1000 acres in Chester River; another conveying 500 acres in the same place to William Rogers of Va. Made 16 Mar. 1679. Sig: John Washbourne, Clerk of Accomac County, Va.

050 20 Nov. 1678 Capt. William Hemsley's acknowledgment of a deed to John Parsons. Daniell Jenifer of "Gargaphell" in Accomack Co., Colony of Va., Gent., to John Parsons of the said County and colony, Planter - 1000 acres in the Province of Maryland in Chester River in Talbot County neare the head of the southeast branch - patented by Daniel Jenifer 10 June 1661 - lately in the tenure and occupation of Daniel Jenifer. Wit: Jn. P. Gence of Va., John Sturgis, Ben. Eyre.

052 16 Mar. 1679 Daniel Jenifer and Ann his wife to William Hemsley - P/A in Talbot County Court to acknowledge sale of 500 acres to William Rogers of Accomack Co., Va. 20 Jan. last past. Received in Accomac Co. Court Mar. 26, 1680. Sig: John Washbourne, Clerk.

21.

052 16 Mar. 1679 Ann, wife of Daniell Jenifer of Accomack County, to William
Anderson of Accomack - P/A. Wit: Tho. Welbourne, Roger Mickells.

053. 20 Jan. 1679 Daniel Jenifer to William Rogers of Accomac Co., Va. -
500 acres in Chester River, Talbot County, on Island Creek - called
"Land of Prophecy" - patented 9 May 1665 - adjoining the land of Andrew
Skinner and Nathaniel Evetts. Wit: John Sturgis, Ben. Eyre.

055 14 Aug. 1681 Sarah Bartlett, wife of Nicholas Bartlett, to Richard
Sweatman - P/A. Wit: Barnard Hodges, J. Barkhead.

056 16 Aug. 1681 Nicholas Bartlett, Planter, and Sarah his wife, to William
Esterson of Talbot, Mariner - 150 acres in Tredhaven Creek, adjoining
"The Exchange" - called "Petty France." Wit: Tho. Vaughn, Thos. Impey.

058 16 Aug. 1681 John Burrows, Planter, to Henry Willcocks - 100 acres in
Island Creek, Chester River, called "Mt. Hope." Wit: William Pawson,
John Parsons.

058 16 Aug. 1681 John Clymer to Daniel Ingerson and Henry Snowden - 200
acres called "Grantam" - adjoining the land laid out for Thomas Williams
on the south side Williams' Branch. Wit: Robert Smith, Henry Pratt.

060 _____ 1681 Henry Pratt and Seath his wife, to Daniel Ingerson and
Henry Snowden - 120 acres called "Wilton" - adjoining land sold to Ed-
ward Baraclift. Wit: Leonard Daniell, John Harker. A bond given by
Pratt witnessed by Thomas Bruff and Robert Smith.

062 24 Dec. 1681 Edward Fuller, Planter, to Robert Hawkshaw - 100 acres on
south side Chester River, "Collington." Wit: Robert Smith, Hugh Sherwood.

063 21 June 1681 Richard Collins and Sarah his wife, to Andrew Hamelton,
Taylor - one-half part or moiety of "Freshford" on the south side Ches-
ter River - granted to John Broadrib - 250 acres. Wit: John Hollins,
Henry Parker.

063 21 June 1681 Robert Hawkshaw and Margaret his wife, to Thomas Carman -
100 acres on south side of the southeast branch Chester River - part of
300 acres - 150 acres of the same formerly belonging to Alexander Maxfield. Wit: John Elliott, Will. Austin.

065 20 Feb. 1681 Edward Stevenson of Wye River and Lettice his wife, to
Samuel Smith of Wye River, Gent. - 200 acres in Wye River called "Bodell"
the dwelling plantation of Stevenson - adjoining land laid out for Thos.
Wilkinson. Wit: Michael Turbutt, James Sedgwick, Rich. Royston.

068 19 Sept. 1681 Mary Hackett wife of Michaell Hackett to James Sedgwick -
P/A to acknowledge a sale to William Sparkes. Wit: Henry Willcockes,
John Burrows.

069 16 Aug. 1681 Michael Hackett and Mary his wife to William Sparkes -
100 acres in Chester River adjoining John Hawkins - sold by Jno. Mitchell.
Wit: Hen. Willcocks, John Parsons.

page

070   19 Sept. 1681   Michael Hackett and Mary his wife, to William Sparkes -
350 acres in Chester River called "Sparkes' Choice." Wit: Henry Willcockes, John Burrows.

072   7 April 1681   Andrew Price in Wye River, Carpender, to Robert Ellis in
Chester River - P/A to recover his debts. Wit: John Glendining, Richard Miresch.

072   20 Sept. 1681   Stephen Tully to Andrew Price - 300 acres, "Tully's Lott"
on the south side of Pearle's Creek. Wit: Robt. Smith, John Davis.

075   21 June 1681   Humphrey Davenport, Chirurgion, to William Warrilowe -
land at the mouth of Broad Creeke - runs to Haleing Creek - part of a
tract formerly granted to Charles Hollingsworth adjoining the land of
Andrew Tootle south side St. Michael's River - formerly possessed by
Alexander Maxwell. Wit; James Murphy, Tho. Bruff.

076   23 Aug. 1681   John Darby, of Newcastle upon Delaware, Innholder, and
Elizabeth his wife, to Roger Weddall of Talbot Co., Cooper - 470 acres
in Corsica Creek, Chester River, called "Sexton" - adjoining the land
of Thomas Bruffe - patented by William Smith 13 Aug. 1666. Wit: Robert
Smith, John Chase, Ja. Coursey. P/A to William Bishopp of Talbot.

078   15 Nov. 1681   Abraham Hurlock, Planter, to Thomas Reynolds, Planter -
in consideration of six cows and calves, one steere and one heifer -
conveys 200 acres on the branches of the head of Tredhaven Creek adjoining William Sharpe, called 'Abraham's Lott." Wit: John Reynolds,
Richard Harington, Thomas Allcock.

081   15 Nov. 1681   Richard Jones, Jr. to John Robinson - 100 acres, south
side Chester River near the branches of Coursegall Creek, called "Jamaica." Wit: Robert Smith, Richard Jones, John Chaires.

082   27 day 8ber 1681   John Sumner, Carpenter, to William Southbee of Talbot - 300 acres called "Kingstowne" - in King's Creek - being made over
to me in open court by Henry Parker. John Jadwin, Attorney for Sumner.
Wit: Nathaniel Browne, William Coule, John Brace, Jane Haymore.

083   14 Mar. 1680   John Parsons, Planter, and Damarus his wife, to John Offley - 200 acres in Chester River called "Spread Eagle" adjoining the
land of William Burton. Wit: Samuel Randall, William Austin.

084   10 Nov. 1681   Robert Moulder, Carpenter, John Butcher, Planter, and Ruth
his wife, to William Cowell, Planter - 300 acres "Tully's Reserve" -
southeast branch of Coursegall Creek in Chester River. Wit: Henry Greene,
Robert Appletree.

085   10 Nov. 1681   Thomas Smithson, Gent., John Stanley and Judith, his wife,
to James Murphy, Gent. - 200 acres "Arcadia" - northeast branch of
Tredhaven Creek. Wit: Richard Dudley, David Rogers. P/A to James Coursey witnessed by Richard Dudley, David Rogers, Elizabeth Girling, Hannah Cahane.

page

090 17 Jan. 1681 Henry Pratt, Planter, and Seth his wife, to Peter Sides, Planter - 200 acres called "Ye Addition" - adjoining the land of John Wells. Wit: William Tong, Daniell Ingerson.

091 16 Mar. 1681 Humphrey Davenport, Chirurgion, to Robert Paige of Kent Co., Planter - part of "Maiden Point" on south side St. Michael's River. Wit: John Offley, Robert Ellis.

093 31 Dec. 1681 Robert Smith and Ann his wife, to James Coursey - P/A. Wit: Solomon Wright, Thomas Bruff.

093 10 Nov. 1681 Robert Smith, Gent., and Ann his wife, to Hugh Paxton, Planter - 300 acres, "Jones' Fancy" - adjoining land laid out for Matthew Mason and Herbert Craft. Wit: Edw. Tomlins, Mathew Tomlins.

097 10 Nov. 1681 Richard Jones the elder, Planter, and Elizabeth his wife, to John Johnson, Planter - 250 acres on south side Chester River called "Denby" - adjoining land of Henry Parker, a parcel called "Jamaica" and the land of Matthew Ward. Wit: Ja. Coursey, Ri. Lamb, Henry Jackson.

100 8 Nov. 1680 Thomas Loggins, Gent., to Samuel Farmer - one-half part of "Upper Dover" on the north side of Choptank River, in the whole, 300 acres - purchased by John Hodges, Senior, of John Richardson and sold by Richard Royston, Attorney, to Thomas Loggins. Wit: John Waymouth, Ralph Swift.

101 18 Feb. 1681 Thomas Loggins to Samuel Farmer - Bill of Sale. Wit: Robert Fortin, Will. Catherup.

102 18 Feb. 1681 Division of "Dover" for Loggins and Farmer made by Thomas Anderson, Chirurgion and Thomas Hutchinson, Farmer. Wit: Francis Neale and John Gardner. Witnesses to the deed: John Waymouth, Lenard Gening, John Shipard, William Hill.

104 10 Feb. 1681 William Bishopp, Gent., to Walter Jones, Planter - 150 acres, part of a tract of 800 acres laid out for Wm. Bishopp on the south side Chester River - adjoining George Reade, Jacob (x) Jenifer's land, William Rogers and John Broadrib's lands. ("x" indicated an error). Wit: Henry Coursey, Jr., Edward Sweatman, Ja. Coursey.

105 15 Oct. 1681 Thomas Bucknall and Mary his wife, of Ann Arundell County, Planter, to John Bird of Ann Arundell - 200 acres, "Turner's Ridge" in Wye River - granted to Thomas Turner 1669 - adjoining land laid out for Thomas Francis - in ye woods. Wit: James Downes, William Gross.

108 18 Mar. 1682 John Rousby, Gent., and Barbary his wife, to Bryan Omealy, Planter - 270 acres called "Haritton" - east side Miles River adjoining the land of Anthony Griffin. Wit: James Murphy, James Hollis.

111 27 Apr. 1682 Cuthbert Phelps, Planter, and Frances his wife, to Thomas Impey, Gent. - Phelp's dwelling plantation and all adjoining lands, called "Cudlington" - 400 acres on Harris Creek adjoining Gerson Cromwell -

page

111 - also "Cudlington's Addition," 50 acres and "Cudlington's Increase,"
50 acres - adjoining the land of Robert White. Wit: Vincent Lowe, James
Murphy, Michaell Turbutt, Hugh Sherwood.

114 1 May 1682 Cuthbert Phelps to Thomas Impey - Bill of Sale for thirty-
three head of cattle. Wit: Erick Imbertson, Thomas Taylor.

115 20 June 1682 Stephen Tully to Lewis Blangey of Kent County, Gent. -
500 acres, "Upper Deale" on south side Chester River. Wit: James Eustis,
Michaell Turbutt, Louis De Rochebrune.

117 _____ 1682 Thomas Loggins of Talbot, Planter, to John, Thomas and Henry
Henrix the natural sons of my beloved wife Elizabeth, borne to her and
her first husband John Henrix - in consideration of natural and fatherly
affection - 150 acres, "Dover," my now dwelling plantation. Wit: John
Burrell, Robert Bretts.

118 _____ 1679 Johane Wyatt, widow and relict of Timothy Wyatt, Planter, deceased - about to enter into a state of matrimony with Walter Quinton of
Talbot, Carpenter - deed of gift to her infant son Timothy, five months
old: 4 cows with calves, 1 young breeding mare, 1 good flock bed with
bolster with a rug, 1 pair blankets and sheets; when he is twenty-one
or at eighteen in case of my death. Wit: Walter Quinton, William Bexley, William Crosse.

119 _____ 1682 John Edmondson, Merchant, to Thomas Hutchinson, Tanner -
200 acres where Hutchinson now dwelleth - bought under the seal of Samuel
Cooke, heir of Miles Cooke and of Henry and William Coursey, Gents., At-
torneys for the widow of Miles Cook - adjoining Emanuell Jenkinson and
Roger Farmer's lands - called "Cooke's Mannor." Wit: James Sedgwick,
John Mullikin.

121 20 June 1682 Henry Fox, Planter, and Hester his wife, to William Hemp-
stead of Talbot, planter - 1000 acres on Marshy Creek in the Northeast
Bay of Chesapeake Bay, taken up by Henry Fox and Philip Land, called
"The Wading Place." Wit: Robt. Collson, T. Delehay.

123 10 June 1682 Robert Ellis, Plaisterer, and Harley his wife, to John
Glendenning of Talbot, Planter - 150 acres between Wye River and Chester
River near ye horse road - called "Forsett's Plaines." Mentions Thomas
Forsett, deceased. Wit: William Tonge, John Johnson.

125 22 Mar. 1681/82 William Stephens to John Cox - 50 acres, "Spring Close,"
north side Choptank River, head of Island Creek - adjoining land laid
out for Patrick Mullicin. Wit: Richard Whitbey, Samuel Hatton.

126 21 June 1681 John Stanley, Merchant, to Thomas Hutchinson, Tanner -
400 acres called "Salisbury Plaine" nigh Tuckahoe Creek - adjoining land
laid out for John Edmondson and Capt. Philemon Lloyd - patented to John
Richardson; sold to Edward Williams and by Williams to Robert Turner in
1673 and given by him in his will to the children of William _(blank)_
begat with his wife Sarah, now known as Sarah Eastgate and sold to John
Stanley. Wit: George Robins, John Hollins.

page

129 20 June 1682 Henry Pratt, Planter, and Seth his wife, to William Young, Carpenter - "The Addition" laid out for Thomas Williams on the east side of Williams' Branch. Wit: James Downes, William Tonge.

131 18 Sept. 1682 Henry Parker, Gent., to Abraham Hurlock - "Parker's Thickett," on west side St. Michael's River on Hunting Creek - adjoining land laid out for John Kinnimont called "The Addition" - containing 50 acres. Wit: Thomas Bowdell, Tho. Bruff.

132 15 Aug. 1682 Richard Dudley, Taylor, and Elinor his wife, to Samuell Broadway, Planter - 200 acres on the west side of Tuckahoe Creek adjoining the land of Thomas Hammond - called "Dudley." Wit: John Pooley, Thomas Vaughn. Acknowledged by Henry Parker before Wm. Coursey, Edward Man and George Robotham.

133 20 June 1682 Richard Dudley, Taylor, and Elinor his wife, to William Jump, Planter - 100 acres on the east side of Tuckahoe Creek by the road leading to St. Jones - called "Pokedy Ridge." Wit: Richard Swetnam, John Pooley.

135 10 June 1682 Hugh Paxton, Planter, and Grace his wife, to John Ponder, Planter - 100 acres, part of "Jones' Fancy" purchased by Paxton from Robert Smith - in Chester River. Wit: Ja. Coursey, John Prince, Thomas Phinney.

139 12 Aug. 1682 William Young, Carpenter, with consent of my wife Frances, to John Browne - part of the land laid out for Thos. Williams called "Ye Addition" on Williams' Branch, Back Wye River - purchased of Henry Pratt. Another adjoining called "Partnership," total in both 350 acres. Wit: Thomas Stevenson, Henry Parker.

142 18 June 1682 Matthew Benham of Kent Co. and Margrett his wife, to Sibella Broadribb - 200 acres called "Stoke," on south side Chester River adjoining land laid out for Samuel Winslow, now in possession of Sibella Broadribb. Wit: Nic. Clouds, Robt. Sadler.

144 16 Jan. 1681 Samuel Farmer, Planter, and Elizabeth his wife, to Thomas Sevill of Talbot - one-half of 150 acres, being 75 acres, of a 300-acre tract called "Upper Dover" - north side Choptank River - purchased by John Hodges, Sr. of John Richardson and sold by Richard Royston, Atty. for Hodges to Thomas Loggins. Wit: Thos. Anderson, John Pooley.

147 15 Aug. 1682 Edward Barraclift, Millwright, and Ann his wife, to Daniel Ingerson and Henry Snoden, Planters - 11 acres, part of "Wilton" at the head of Wye River - in consideration of work done by Ingerson and Snoden to the dam of the mill of Edward Barraclift - adjoins the land called "Grantam." Wit: Jon. Sargeant, Benjamin Blofeld.

150 10 Aug. 1678 Thomas Roe to John Dams - his moiety of "Hambleton's Park," sold 16 Dec. 1678 by George Cowley and Ann his wife to Roe and Damos - 137 acres on west side of a branch of Wye River, lately in the tenure of John Slather, deceased and now occupied by Roe and Dams.

page

adjoining the land of John Wright called "Scipton" – granted by John Scott and Margaret his wife to George Cowley and Edward Norman. Wit: Richard Jones, Tho. Bruff, Ja. Coursey.

153 1 Oct. 1682 Ralph Ellston, Sr., Planter, to son-in-law Zorababel Wells – gift of 100 acres called "Thief Keep Out" on Second Creek. Wit: Tho. Impey, Ralph Ellston, Jr., Thomas Tucker.

154 10 Mar. 1682 Humphrey Davenport, Chyrurgion, to William Warrilowe, Cooper – Bond. Wit: James Murphy, Thos. Smithson.

154 21 Sept. 1682 Richard Gould, Planter, with consent of my wife, Ursula, to Peter Haddaway, Planter – 100 acres of land on the Eastern Shore adjoining the land of Gresham Cromwell – first purchased by Alexander Macotter and Daniel Glover. Wit: Richard Royston, John Whittington.

155 20 June 1682 Lewis Closier, Cooper, and Susana his wife, to William Anderson – 150 acres at head of St. Michael's Creek, called "Knapp's Lott." Wit: Jos. Atkins, Jno. Baynard, Jno. Ayres.

156 22 Nov. John Breame, Planter, and Mary his wife, to James Smith of Talbot – 150 acres on Hambleton's Creek, called "Jamaica." Wit: Robert Smith, Richard Gould.

157 3 Nov. 1681 John Breame and Mary his wife to Thomas Wetherby and William Hackett, Carpenters – P/A to convey "Jamaica" and also a parcel sold to Peter Haddaway called "Ashton" on Hambleton's Creek. Wit: Richard Gould, Jonas Greenwood.

158 23 Nov. 1681 John Breame and Mary his wife, to Peter Haddaway, Carpenter – 300 acres called "Ashton" on Hambleton's Creek – to be divided into 150 acres – taken up by Stephen Tully and sold to John Breame. Wit: Robt. Smith, Richard Gould.

159 23 Nov. 1681 Bond given by Breame witnessed by Richard Gould and Jonas Greenwood.

159 16 Nov. 1682 Christopher Santee, Planter, and Anne his wife, to Thomas Roe, Planter – 200 acres om the south side Wye River adjoining Simon Stevens' "Stevens' Plaines" – called "Christopher's Lott." Wit: William Hatfield, Robert Mynott.

162 8 Sept. 1682 Richard Jackson, son and heir of Richard Jackson, deceased, to his brother, William Jackson – 300 acres of land and the dwelling plantation of their father, according to the deceased's last will and testament devising the same to his youngest son. Wit: Richard Mirax, Thomas Thompson, George Smith, Ralph Abbott, Ja. Coursey.

162 16 Sept. 1682 John Preston, Planter, and Joan his wife, to Charles Dickinson of Talbot, Planter – "Hatton," 600 acres purchased of George Cowley and Anne his wife, and Richard Richardson. Wit: Edward Man, William Combes, T. Delehay.

page

163 10 Jan. 1682 Henry Coursey the younger, Gent., to Peter Sayer, Gent. -
by Power of Attorney granted by Robert Morris of Ratcliff, Parrish of
Stepney, County Middlesex (Eng.), Mason and Mariner - 400 acres on Wye
River called "Mount Mill" - granted 1665 to Robert Morris. Wit: Jona.
Sybury, Thomas Vaughan, James Coursey. Witnesses to P/A were James Cona-
way and William Hill.

165 20 Nov. 1682 Thomas Smithson, John Stanley, and Judith, wife of John
Stanley - by their Attorney Griffith Jones - to Charles and Samuel
Lewes of Talbot, planters - 100 acres called "Cumberland" - adjoining
Edmondson's "Clifton." Wit: John Baynard, James Bishop.

166 15 Jan. 1682 Robert Smith and Ann his wife - by their Attorney Matthew
Tomlins - to John Stark - "Bradbourne's Delight," 200 acres on Coursi-
gall Creek adjoining land laid out for W. Hemsley now in possession of
Matthais Peterson. Wit: Will. Bonham, Mathew Thomlins, Thomas Gough.
P/A witnessed by Ri. Twiggs and William Hinson.

168 15 Jan. 1682 Gertrude, John and Francis Anderton to Zorababel Wells -
"Birchley" on Second Creek. Wit: James Dowdell, Henry Costin, John
Hawkins. Gertrude Anderton, widdow, to her son John Anderton - P/A.
Wit: James Dowdell, William Powell.

169 20 Mar. 1682 Richard Peacock, Gent., to Daniel Joaes (Joads or Toas?)
of Durham Co., England, Mariner - "Sarah's Joynture" in Cecil County at
the head of a branch of Bohemia River - begins at a white oak beside
Abbaquimany path - being the first bounded tree of land laid out for
James Murphy called "Skillton," surveyed 13 Sept. last - containing 600
acres of land. Wit: James Benson, Edw. Elyott.

170 20 Mar. 1682 James Murphy, Gent., and Mary his wife, to Daniel Jeves,
(Joads, Joaes or Toas) of the County and Bishoprick of Durham, England -
"Skelton," upon the branches of the Bohemia River adjoining "Stockton,"
laid out for Thomas Vaughn - begins at an oak beside Abaquimmony Path -
surveyed 13 Sept. last. Wit: Thos. Vaughn, Michaell Turbutt, Edward
Elyott.

172 19 July 1682 James Murphy, Gent., and Mary his wife, to John Hamor,
Planter - 200 acres on the northeast branch of Tredhaven Creek called
"Arcadia." Wit: Tho. Jordan, Jos. Hall.

out of sequence

171 20 Mar. 1682 Thomas Vaughn and Susan his wife, to Daniel Joaes (Joce,
Joads, Jeves?) of Durham Co., Eng. - "Stockton," on Bohemia River in
Cecil County. Wit: James Benson, Michaell Turbutt, Edw. Ellitt.

173 Last Feb. 1682 John Hamor, Planter, and Anna his wife, dweller in Talbot,
to Jasper Hall - 50 acres, "Prevention" - adjoining land of Josiah Lambert on the south - 50 acres, "Wharton," on southeast branch Second
Creek in Choptank River. Wit: James Murphy, Thos. Jordan.

174 3 Mar. 1682 Emanuel Jenkinson, Planter, and Elizabeth his wife, to
George Royston of Calvert Co., Planter - 300 acres, "Beginning," on
Choptank River. Wit: Thos. Smithson, John Stanley.

page
175 25 Dec. 1682 William Mountikue, Attorney for Peter Willson and his wife
Elizabeth of Cecil Co., Planter, to George Palmer of Talbot, Planter -
200 acres called "Spread Eagle" - mentions Daniel Jenifer and John Parsons. Wit: John Whittington, James Smith, Daniel Carnell. Witness to
P/A: John Dine.

178 10 Nov. 1682 Thomas Smithson, John Stanley and Judith Stanley his wife,
to Edmund Fish, Planter - 120 acres called "Gatterly Moore" on Tredhaven
Creek. Wit: Edward Man, William Combes.

179 1 Dec. 1682 Daniel Carnell, Freeman, to Robert Hopper of Scarborough,
England, Mariner - 500 acres called "Yorkshire," on the east side of
Susquehaunough River in Cecil County - adjoining "Sinclare's Purchase"
laid out for Dominick Inglish and "Mt. Arraratt," laid out for Henry
Hazlewood. Wit: George Gaskill, Hadaweyen Whitfield, Richard Mitchell.
P/A to Bryan Omealy witnessed by Richard Mitchell, John Careless, Abra-
ham Morgan.

181 8 Jan. 1682 John Edmondson, Merchant, to William Johnson of London,
England, Mariner - in consideration of a marriage already solemnized
between William Johnson and Sarah Edmondson, daughter of John Edmondson
and Sarah his wife - 900 acres of land on the northeast side of the main
branch of Thirdhaven Creek called the freshes main branch - purchased
of Francis Armstrong, Sr., since deceased, and now in the tenure of
Stephen Cady. Wit: Griffith Jones, Robert Webb.

182 15 Nov. 1682 William Sharpe and Elizabeth his wife, to William Wintersell, Planter - 300 acres called "Sharpe's Chance" adjoining "Londonderry." Wit: Jos. Attkins, Jno. Salter.

183 20 Mar. 1682 John Lillingston and Mary his wife - by Mr. Richard Jones,
Sr. - to Thomas Wyatt - 200 acres called "Barkes" adjoining "Ward Parke."
Wit: Simon Willmer, Jno. Stephens.

185 20 Mar. 1682 Thomas Wyatt and Judith his wife - by Michael Hackett -
to John Nicholson - 100 acres, part of a tract purchased fron John
Lillingston, adjoining "Ward Parke." Wit: Roger Burras, Elizabeth
Burras. Witness to Judith Wyatt's P/A: John Parsons, John Sparkes.

187 20 Mar. 1682 Humphrey Davenport of Talbot, Chyrurgion, to Daniel Joads
(Joaes, Jeves) of the County and Bishoprick of Durham, England - 600
acres, "Hembry" in Kent County, north side Chester River. Wit: Joseph
Semphill, Daniel Carnell.

188 3 Mar. 1682 Anthony Mayle and Mary his wife, to John Salter - 200 acres
called "Plaine Dealing" on Choptank River in the western branch of Tredhaven Creek, in a small creek called Halling Creek - also 50 acres called
"Wyatt's Fortune" on the eastern side of "Plaine Dealing." Wit: John
Stanley, Jos. Atkins.

191 25 Oct. 1681 Col. Lemuell Mason and his wife Ann of Elizabeth River
Parish, Lower Norfolk Co., Va. - sole heirs of Mr. Henry Sewell, Mer-

chant, to Charles Egerton of Elizabeth River Parish - 700 acres in Choptank River called "Mt. Hope;" also 100 acres, "Upper Range" - assigned
to Sewell (since deceased) by John Edmondson and his wife Sarah. Wit:
William Parren, William Vaughn, William Dundas. Charles Edgerton to
John Edmondson - assignment.

192 18 Dec. 1682 Anne Mason, wife of Lemuell Mason, being disabled to come
to County Court to acknowledge the deed of sale, Capt. William Robinson,
Major Anthony Lawson, Mr. Henry Spratt and Mr. George Newton, four of his
Majestie's Justices of the Peace, Lower Norfolk County, at the request of
Mason and Edgerton met at the house of Col. Mason to take her acknowledg-
ment. William Porton, Clerk, County of Norfolk.

193 7 Mar. 1682 Edward Stevenson, Planter, and Lettice his wife, to Dr. Wm.
Hemsley of Talbot - land conveyed to Stevenson by Thomas Emerson and his
wife Katherine, 29 April 1678. Wit: John Michell, Robert Collson.

193 26 Mar. 1682 William Hemsley, Gent., to Thomas Emerson, Planter - 500
acres on an island in Wye River, called "Newark Upon Trent." Wit: Wm.
Finney, Jos. Semphill.

194 17 Apr. 1683 Henry and William Coursey, Gents., and Samuel Cooke, Marin-
er, son and heir of Miles Cook, to John Edmondson, Merchant - "Mannor of
Cook's Hope," 1000 acres in Tredhaven Creek - willed by Miles Cook to
Dorothy his wife and conveyed by her to the Courseys. Wit: Phil. Lloyd,
Tho. Vaughn, James Coursey; James Coursey, atty. for Samuel Cook.

199 15 June 1683 William Young, Carpender, and Francis his wife, to Richard
Jones, Smith - 100 acres, "Young's Chance" on Back Wye River - adjoining
the land of Hugh Paxton - "Ditteridge," laid out for Richard Bridges -
and land laid out for Matthew Mason. Wit: James Sedgwick, Tho. Emerson.

201 13 June 1683 John Edmondson, Merchant, to Emmanuel Jenkinson, Merchant -
300 acres on the road from John Edmondson's to Dover, at the head of
Stoney Branch - adjoining the land of Robert Bryant. Wit: Robert Boreman, Walter Quinton, Robert Webb.

204 19 June 1683 Henry Pratt, Planter, and Seth his wife, to Peter Sides -
350 acres called "The Addition" at the head of Wye River. Wit: Benjamin
Blofeld, Thomas Bruff.

205 22 June 1683 George Allemby, Planter, to Christopher Battson of Talbot,
Cooper - 50 acres on Michaels Creek called "Willingbrow." Mention James
Scott. Wit: Henry Newman, Emanuel Jenkinson.

205 7 June 1683 Robert Bryan and Lydia his wife to John Price, Bricklayer -
100 acres, "Hatfield" and "Hatfield's Addition" - begins at an oak near
Bryan's dwelling house. Wit: John Wiles, Thos. Hutchinson.

207 19 June 1683 Stephen Tully and John Robinson, Planters, to Matthew Smith -
200 acres, "Content" on the north side of a small branch on the west
side Tuckahoe Creek. Sig: Ann Robson. Wit: Jno. Sargeant, Simon Stevens.
Bond given to Smith signed by Stephen Tully and John Robson.

page

209 19 June 1683. Stephen Tully and John Robinson, Planters, to Simon
Steevens - one-half of 600 acres called "Providence" - on a branch of
Tuckahoe Creek. Wit: Peter Sydes, Jno. Sargeant, Jno Clemans.
Sig: Ann Robson.

212 9 June 1683. John Robinson, Carpenter, and Ann his wife, to John Sargeant, Carpenter - "Robinsons Farm" on a branch of Tuckahoe Creek adjoining "Tully's Addition" formerly laid out for Stephen Tully. Wit:
Stephen Tully, Peter Sydes, Hen. Gill.

213 17 Oct. 1682 William Tilghman, Gent., to Zachariah Tompson, Taylor -
250 acres in Talbot County, south side Chester River - part of 1000
acres caid out for William Tilghman and Francis Shepheard called
"Guilford." Wit: Jeoffrey Mattershaw, Thomas Cross. Bond given by
Tilghman witnessed by Thos. Collins and Robert Spencer.
Mary Tilghman for and behalf of her sone, William Tilghman, came before this court and acknowledged this deed of sale to Z. Tompson.

215 18 Oct. 1682 Zara Tompson to William Tilghman - note for 2000 lbs of
tobacco on demand and 1500 more on 10 October next; and 1500 more on
10 Oct. 1684, being three several bills dated 17 Oct. 1682. Wit:
Thomas Collins, Robert Spencer.

215 21 Aug. 1683 John Edmondson, Merchant, to John Stanley, Gent. - land
near the dwelling plantation of Stanley - 90 acres called "Cook's
Hope" on the northeast side of a branch of Tredaven Creek - part of
"Cook's Hope" laid out for Michaell Cooke and adjoining another laid
out for Job Nutt. Wit: James Benson, Thomas Smithson.

215 20 Aug. 1683 Andrew Hambleton, Taylor, and Jane his wife, to Thomas
Bee - 125 acres, part of "Freshford" on a branch of Island Creek, Ches-
ter River - bought of Richard Collins. Wit: Hen. Willcockes, Andrew
Price, Jno. Tillison.

218 10 July 1683. George Robins and Margaret his wife, to Edward Barrowclift, Millwright and Benjamin Blofeld, Planter - "Hildson," between
the heads of the branches of Tuckahoe Creek and Wye River - surveyed
25 June 1679 for 200 acres. Wit; James Benson, Robert Gouldesburgh,
James Causey.

221 15 Aug. 1683 George Robins, Gent., and Margarett his wife, to John
Turner, Planter - 100 acres, part of "Gouldesbrough" - adjoining the
land of Richard Jennings - the remaining part not sold to Walter Quinton and John Squires. Wit: Edward Man, William Combes.

224 21 Aug. 1683 John Lane, Planter, and Mary his wife, to Joseph Hicks -
150 acres, "Charleville" - near the branches of Tuckahoe Creek. Wit:
T. Delehay, Daniell Carnell.

225 7 Sept. 1683 George Robins and Margarett his wife, to Walter Quinton - a moiety of "Gouldesbrough" - in the whole 400 acres improved,
late in the tenure of Walter Quinton - on the north side Choptank
River at the head of the eastern branch of Tredhaven Creek - the first

page

tree at the head of the branch and Bullingbrooke road - 150 acres. Wit: Edward Dalton, Daniel Carnell. Margarett Robins acknowledges before William Combes.

227 10 Sept. 1683 William Gross, Gent., and Hester his wife, to Richard Sweatnam, Carpenter - 200 acres, a moiety of land laid out for Roger Grosse, Gent., called "Abington" near the eastern branch of Wye River - southeast side of Richard Winn's land which is the other part. Wit: Thomas Vaughn, James Sedgwick, James Coursey.

230 21 Aug. 1683 Joseph Hicks, Planter, to Emanuel Jenkinson, Merchant - whereas John Squires by indenture dated 9 Nov. 1681 to Joseph Hicks conveyed 150 acres called "Gouldesbrough" at the head of the eastern branch of Tredhaven Creek - this indenture, in consideration of 400 lbs. of tobacco and 150 acres of other land called "Charleville" on a branch of Tuckahoe Creek (granted to John Lane 25 Jan. 1681), which Lane sold to Emanuel Jenkinson; the said John Lane and Mary his wife at the request of Jenkinson and with the consent of Joseph Hicks have granted to Joseph Hicks the above 150 acres called "Charleville." Wit: T. Delehay, Daniell Carnell.

232 20 Jan. 1682 George Watts, Sr. to George Prouse of Dorchester, Planter - with Ann Watts, his wife - consideration of a man servant and 3 barrells of Indian Corn - 200 acres called "Beare Poynt" in the northeast branch of Great Choptank River on the western side of the branch, adjoining John Ingram. Wit: Thos. Smithson, John Stanley.

233 10 Nov. 1683 Francis Sheppard, Planter, and Hannah his wife, to Hugh Johnson, Planter - 500 acres in Chester River, Talbot County - a moiety or half of 1000 acres called "The Beginning" - formerly laid out for William Tilghman, Gent. and Francis Sheppard in joynt tenancy.

236 20 Nov. 1683 Stephen Tulley, Planter, to Simon West of Talbot, Planter - 200 acres called "Stepheny" on the west side of the northernmost main branch of Tuckaho Creek - adjoining "Tulley's Addition" formerly laid out for Stephen Tulley. Wit: Solomon Wright, Nath. Wright.

238 10 Sept. 1683 John Donne, Planter, to Simon Harris, Planter - with consent of Margarett Donne his wife - 200 acres, "Donne's Range," at the head of Brewer's Branch, Wye River. Wit: Moses Harris, John Emerson.

240 20 Nov. 1682 William Kircum and Alice his wife, to William Purnell - 200 acres, "Kircum's Lott" between the northeast branch of Choptank River and Tuckaho. Wit: John Lane, Daniel Morrihy. P/A to John Lane.

242 20 Nov. 1683 John Robinson, Carpenter, and Anne his wife, to Thomas Pune - 100 acres (part of 600 acres) called "Providence" - taken up by Stephen Tulley and John Robinson and by them divided - on the west side of the northernmost main branch of Tuckaho Creek adjoining Henry Gill's 100 acres out of the same. Wit: Stephen Tulley, Simon West.

page
244 20 Nov. 1683 Anne Robinson to Richard Sweatnam - P/A to acknowledge
a deed made by John Robinson, my husband, to Thomas Pune for 100 acres
called "Providence" and 200 acres between John Robinson and John Gatterly called "Chestnut Meadows." Wit: St. Tulley, Hen. Gill.

245 18 Dec. 1683 Richard Royston, Gent., and Mary his wife, to Richard
Sweatnam, Gent. - 600 acres in Chester River, a moiety or half of 1200
acres called "Royston" patented 1 Aug. 1673 - the other moiety formerly sold to Simon Irons, 23 Mar. 1674. Wit: Thomas Impey, James Benson.
Richard Royston acknowledges this deed before Edward Man, James Murphey. Wit: Thomas Impey, Clerk.

248 14 Jan. 1683/4 Vincent Lowe, Esq. and Elizabeth Lowe his wife, to
Charles Hollinsworth an inhabitant of Talbot County - 300 acres called
"Brimington" on the south side Chester River adjoining the land of Geo.
Read - patented 20 June 1677. Wit: George Robins, William Combes.

250 15 Jan. 1683/4 Robert Collson of Talbot, Planter, to Lawrence Knowles,
Kingdom of Ireland, Gent. - 100 acres, "Folley" - south side St. Michaell's River - adjoining "Rich Neck." Wit: James Murphey, Sam. Skip-
well, William Snelling. Acknowledged by Robert Collson before Vincent
Lowe and James Murphey. Test: Tho. Impey, Clk.

251 15 Jan. 1683 William Hatfield, Planter, and Elizabeth his wife, to John
Thrift, Planter - 150 acres called "Normanton" in the woods near the
head of a branch of Wye River called the Bread and Cheese Harbour Branch.
Wit: John Sargeant, Step. Tulley.

253 16 da, 3 mo called May, 1681 John Judwin of Talbot to William Southbee,
Thomas Taylor, Henry Parrott and John Wotters - with consent and behalf
of himself and partners - 1 acre of a tract I now live upon - for the
use of the Quakers - to meet upon, build a meeting house and bury their
dead. Wit: Thomas Peterson, John Yate, John Estell, Thomas Errington.

255 15 Jan. 1683 Vincent Lowe, Esq. and Elizabeth his wife, to Edward Elli-
ot, Planter - 500 acres called "Slaughterton" in Talbot, south side of
Chester River in the woods by a fresh run called Rousby'es Branch - adjoining land laid out for Christopher Rousby. Wit: Tho. Impey, James
Sedgwick.

256 15 Jan. 1683 Vincent Lowe, Esq., and Elizabeth his wife, to Edward Elliott - 500 acres, "Lowe's Desire" - south side Chester River, north side
Red Lyon Branch - adjoining land laid out for John Slaughter (the whole
1500 acres - pat'd. to Vincent Lowe 10 Aug. 1683.) Wit: Tho. Impey,
James Sedgwick.

258 18 Mar. 1683 William Young, Carpenter, and Frances his wife, to Edward Tomlins, Planter - 200 acres on the main branch of Back Wye River
called "Young's Chance" - adjoining "Mt. Mill" laid out for Robert Morris. Wit: John Glendenning, Daniel Normanton, John Willson.

33.

page
260 16 Oct. 1683 William Crump and Frances his wife, to James Barber, both
inhabitants of Talbot County - 200 acres, "Plaine Dealing" on south side
Chester River - west side of Broadrib's Branch. Wit: John Hix, Thomas
Millbourn.

262 25 Feb. 1683/4 William Crump and Frances his wife, to William Jones -
150 acres, "Crump's Chance" on a branch of Island Creek, Chester River,
called Broadrib's Branch. Wit: John Hix, Thos. Millbourn.

264 18 Dec. 1683 John Barwick of Wye River, Planter, to William Crosse -
a moiety of "Normanton," 100 acres in tenure of William Crosse - on a
branch of Wye River. Wit: Thos. Anderson, Robt. Gouldesburgh.

263 23 Feb. 1683/4 Alexander Jordaine, Planter, to Christopher Pinder -
with consent of Mary, wife of A. Jordaine - 100 acres called "Jordain's
Folley" on the north side Great Choptank River, west side of Harris
Creek - taken up by A. Jordain. Wit: Ralph Dawson, Francis Anderton.

269 26 Feb. 1683 William Finney, Planter, to my daughter Mary Semphill and
her husband, Joseph Semphill, Chyrurgian - wedding gift - a plantation
on the branches of Wye River - occupied by William Watkins under a lease.
Wit: James Sedgwick, John Salter, George Hurlock.

270 12 Feb. 1683 John Parsons of Kent County, Province of Maryland, Plan-
ter, to Richard Burkett of Talbot, Planter - 100 acres, part of "Spread
Eagle" - adjoining John Offley's southeast line and the land of Thomas
Seaward. Wit: John Offley, William Hollinsworth. Damaris, wife of
John Parsons, to Thomas Wyatt - P/A. 14 June 1684. Wit: John Offley,
Wm. Hollinsworth.

271 25 Oct. 1683 Richard Jones, Jr., Planter, to John Nab, Cordwainer -
100 acres, "Jones' Fortune" - south side Chester River - adjoining
"Tilghman's Addition" and the lands of Solomon and Nathaniel Wright.
Wit: Robert Smith, Thomas Thurston.

273 26 May 1684 John Stanley and Christopher Baitson, Planters, to Miles
Thornton, Planter - a moiety or half of 100 acres called "Chance" in
Talbot, near the land of Thomas Cox and a branch of Treadhaven called
Thomas Cock's Branch. Wit: Tho. Delehay, Ed. Hargreaves. Acknowledged
by Stanley and Baitson before Edw. Man and Wm. Combes. Judith Stanley,
wife of John, acknowledged before Man and Combes, 26 May 1684.

275 19 Nov. 1683 John Parsons, Carpenter, and Damerous his wife, to John
Haymer - 199 acres in Island Creek, Chester River. Wit: John Jones,
Alexander Deverox. Damerous Parsons to Thomas Wyatt - P/A, 30 Mar.
1683/4. Wit: Henry Willcockes, John Hamer. Bond given by John Parsons
19 Nov. 1683 witnessed by Michaell Hackett and Thomas Wyatt.

277 14 Jan. 1683/4 John Parsons and Damerus his wife, to John Hamer - 50
acres on west side Island Creek, Chester River, called "Highgate" -
adjoining John Hawkins and intersecting with the lands formerly belonging to John Singleton and Thos. Norris. Wit: Matt. Banum, Hugh Mason.

page
278 28 April 1684 William Southbe, Planter, to James Peacocke of Stockton
Upon Lease, County and Bishoprick of Dunstin and Durham, Kingdon of
England, Marriner - 500 acres, "Parker's Park" - granted to Henry Parker 1 Aug. 1673, north side Choptank River, east side of northernmost
branch of King's Creek and sold to William Southbe - where Southbe now
Liveth - with his watermill, hardwares and millpond and all mill pooles,
mill dams, stankes, bankes, ponds, streams, water, water courses, fishing places, wayes and paths, passages, easements, profits, commodities,
advantages, emoluments and appaurtenances whatsoever to the said mill
and a cartway from the aforesaid lands through "Kingston" (containing
300 acres) unto convenient landings in King's Creek. Wit: John Edmondson, Joseph Smith, Daniel Carnell. Joane Southbe, wife of William, releases her dower.

281 Last day of May 1684 Henry Fox and Hester his wife, of St. Michaell's
River, Planter, to James Murphey, Gent. - in conxideration of ₤104 law-
ful money of England; 23000 lbs. of tobacco and 500 acres on Saxifras
Creek called "Mt. Pleasant" and 1000 acres called "Levell Ridge" at the
head of Saxifras River in Cecil County - conveyes land on the east side
of Chesapeake Bay called "Rich Neck" - neare to the Isle of Kent and
respecting that part of the Island called Island Necke - on Southeast
Bay, bounded on the west by Mitchell's Creeke. 1000 acres, granted to
Philip Land and Henry Fox, deceased, by patent ___ Oct. 1651. Wit:
Robert Smith, Francis Armstronge.

282 19 June 1684 Robert Parvis amd Cecilly his wife of New Kent, Province
of Pennsylvania, Taylor, to James Earle of Talbot - 150 acres called
"Highfield" at the head of a small run of Tuckahoe Creek. Wit: Robt.
Beets, Christopher Moore. Bond witnessed by Betts, Moore and William
Purnell.

283 15 June 1684 John Lane and Mary his wife, to George Robotham - 250
acres on a branch of Tuckahoe Creek called "Kingseale" - adjoining
"Boston's Addition." Wit: Wm. Wrench, Wm. Kircum.

284 17 June 1684 Andrew Price and Mary his wife, to Thomas Green - 100
acres, "Liberty" - adjoining the land of John Glendenning and Col. Coursey. Wit: Henry Coursey, Gent., William Coursey.

286 25 Apr. 1684 Henry Clay of Talbot and Mary his wife, to James Sedg-
wick, Gent. - the plantation whereon I now dwell called "Lurkey" - 200
acres near the head of Harris Creek, in Choptank River on the Eastern
Shore - granted to Nicholas Lurkey 2 Aug. 1662. Also 100 acres called
"Clay's Neck" on Cattaile Branch adjoining the land of Henry Clay and
the lands of Zachariah Wade now possessed by William Leeds. Wit: James
Murphy, Griffith Jones. Mary Clay acknowledged before Edward Mann and
William Combes.

288 16 June 1684 Henry Parker to William Grosse - 50 acres, "Newnam's
Fields" - north side St. Michael's River - adjoining land laid out for
Roger Grosse called "Ashby." Wit: Wm. Finney, George Holland.

page
289 10 Nov. 1682 Henry Parker, Gent., to Thomas Bruff, Taylor - 400 acres
on Corsica Creek - "Woodland Necke" and "Woodland Addition" - adjoining the land laid out for John Chayres. Wit: James Coursey, Christopher
Denny, John Johnson. Thomas Bruff and Henry Parker agree that Christopher Denny's lands adjoining shall stand according to patent. Wit: Robt.
Smith, John Aldridge.

292 18 June 1684 James Sedgwick, Gent., to Jacob Seth, Planter - 300 acres
called "Hackney Marsh" in the woods near Thomas' Branch, Wye River -
adjoining William Young's "Middle Plantation" and the land of Robert
Morris called "Mt. Mill." Wit: John Woodward, John Heartley. Acknowledged in open court before Vincent Lowe and Edward Mann, Justices.

293 16 June 1684 Cornelius Mullrayne, Planter, to Francis Chappline, Planter - 500 acres called "Broad Oake" on west side Bullingbrooke Creek,
north side Great Choptank River. Wit: Thomas Hutchinson, Nicholas
Haggitt, Charles Marham.

295 18 Mar. 1683 Peter Hadaway to Thomas Forde, Planter - 150 acres, a
moiety of "Ashton" in Talbot County, south side Chester River - adjoining land laid out for Stephen Tulley and the land of Thomas Wetherby.
Wit: Thomas Collins, Thomas Collner.

296 7 June 1684 Henry Pratt, Planter, and Seth his wife, to John Pursell,
Cooper - 200 acres of land adjoining "Wilton." Wit: Wm. Finney, Wm.
Younge, John Clemmons.

299 6 Nov. 1683 Thomas Wyatt and Judith his wife, to John Parsons - 199
acres on Island Creek, Chester River. Wit: John Burrowes, Richard
Bridges. Bond witnessed by John Hamer and Michael Hackett.

301 16 da, 3rd month called May 1684 William Southbe, late of Talbot,
Boatwright, to John Ashdell, Tanner - 200 acres out of a patent for 300
acres called "Kingston" - in King's Creek on the east side of the northeast branch - adjoining John Ashdell's plantation. Wit: John Juell,
John (JB - his marke) .

302 14 June 1684 Henry Parker, Gent., to Michaell Russell, Planter - part
of "Fishing Bay" in St. Michael's River - adjoining James Scott's "The
Addition" and opposite to the plantation of William Bush. Wit: Daniell
Wallker, Abraham Hurlocke.

304 17 June 1684 Jacob Seth, Planter, and Barbara his wife, to William
Younge, Carpenter - 33 acres, part of "Mt. Mill" formerly laid out for
Robert Morris - west side of Thomas' Branch. Wit: Wm. Coursey, Andrew
Price.

306 10 Mar. 1683 John Parsons, Planter, County of Kent, Province of Maryland, to Thomas Seaward of the same place, Planter - 300 acres, a moiety
of "Spread Eagle" - adjoining Richard Burkett. Dameras, wife of John
Parsons gives consent. Wit: Robert Boreman, John Hussi.

page

308 14 Mar. 1680 John Parsons, Planter, and Damarus, his wife, to William Burton, Planter - 200 acres, part of "Spread Eagle" near the head of the southeast branch of Chester River. Wit: John Jones, Alexander Deverex.

309 17 Mar. 1683/4 Damerus Parsons to Thomas Wyatt - P/A to acknowledge the above deed. Wit: Henry Willcockes, John Hamer.

310 17 June 1684 James Sylvester of Talbot, Planter, and Elizabeth his wife, to Thomas Bradshaw and John Bradshaw, Planters - 100 acres called "Sylvester's Chance" on north side Great Choptank River, east side of Tuckahoe Creek - near the land laid out for Seth Garratt. Wit: John Lane, Joseph Wiggott.

312 19 June 1683 Francis Sheppheard and Anne his wife, to Thomas Wetherby - 200 acres called "Sheppheard's Hooke" in a fork of a branch of Double Creeke, south side Chester River. Wit: Robt. Mackline, Nic. Cloudes.

314 10 July 1683 Arthur Emory, Planter, to Arthur, my eldest sonne, for his natural life and to his heirs - all that dwelling house and plantation where he now dwelleth and 300 acres of land belonging called "Batchelor's Chance"on the fresh runs of Wye River - also 100 acres on southeast side of the branch adjoining the said 300 acres, being one-half of 200 acres called "Butterfield" - formerly purchased of one Gyles Butter - for want of issue of the said Arthur, to the second, third, fourth, fifth, sixth, seventh, eighth, ninth and tenth sonne and/or their heirs, successively. Wit: Wm. Finney, Robert White, James Coursey.

316 16 June 1684 Henry Parker to William Allen now of St. Michael's River - "Parker's Freshes" on north side Choptank River, eastern side of Tuckahoe Creeke - adjoining the land of John Morgan - 300 acres according to patent. Wit: Daniell Wallker, Abraham Hurlocke.

318 14 June 1684 James Sylvester and Elizabeth his wife, to John Lane, Planter - 200 acres called "Golden Lyon" on east side Tuckahoe Creek - lying between "Kircum's Lott" and "Dudley." Wit: Thomas Bradshaw, John Bradshaw.

319 26 Oct. 1682 George Collinson, Cooper, and Elizabeth his wife, to James Dowdell, Planter - 50 acres west side Harris Creek called "Rahobeth's Poynt" adjoining "Rahobeth." Wit: Christopher Pypard, Andrew Sexton, Thomas Lurkey.

322 11 May 1683 William Broadwell of Elizabethtowne, Province of East Jersey, Shoemaker, to Cornelius Mullrayne of Talbot - 500 acres of land at Bullenbrooke in Talbot purchased of Coll. Wm. Collburne of Somersett County. Wit: Wm. Biddle, Elias Farr, Justices in Burlington, Province of West Jersey. Thomas Revell, record these. (sic)

William Coulbourne, Sr. of Somerset Co.'s declaration of sale to Wm. Broadwell of 500 acres called "Broad Oake" - west side Bullingbrooke Creek and since sold by Broadwell to Mullrayne. 1 March 1683/4.

page
Wit: John Wootters, John Sallter, John West, Jacob Loockerman.

323 2 Mar. 1683/4 William Coulbourne to George Roberts - a request to acknowledge at court for Cornelius Mullrayne.

323 1 June 1684 James Murphey, Gent., to Henry Fox, Planter - in consideration of "Rich Neck" deed 1 May by Henry Fox and the sum of five shillings - 150 acres called "Raye's Poynt" - north side Choptank River, on
Hethod's Branch, Second Creek - and 100 acres on south side Second Creek
called "The Enlargement" - adjoining the land of Alexander Ray. Wit:
Robert Smith, Francis Armstronge.

325 1 June 1684 James Murphy, Gent., to Henry Fox, Planter - consideration
"Rich Neck" - 1000 acres in Cecil County on a branch of Saxifras River
called Mill Branch. on Delaware Path - "Levell Ridge." Also 500 acres
called "Mt. Pleasant" - Cecil County at the head of Saxifras Creek.
Wit: Robert Smith, Francis Armstronge.

327 17 June 1684 William Grosse, Planter, to Nathaniel Cleave, Planter -
100 acres, part of a parcel formerly possessed by Roger Grosse, Sr. of
Ann Arrundell County, Planter, called "Ashby" - on St. Michael's River.
Wit: Wm. Harris, John Newnam.

329 19 Aug. 1684 Daniell Walker, Planter, to Abraham Hurlocke - "Woodland
Necke" on the east side of Woodenhawk's Branch of King's Creek - adjoining James Barber's "Somerly" and John Edmondson and Joseph Sone's
called "The Square" - 100 acres by patent. Wit: Henry Parker, Walter
Lyster, Richard Sanders.

331 15 Sept. 1684 Philemon Lloyd of Talbot, Gent., from Henry Parker -
"Ninevah" on the west side of the southwest branch of Corsica Creek -
adjoining the land of Christopher Thomas, patented 20 April 1667 for
600 acres. "Ninevah's Addition," adjoining, 200 acres patented 16 Aug.
1680 - also one-half of "Lloyd Parke" on Tuckahoe Creek - 1000 acres
patented 8 May 1666. Wit: James Clayland, William Leedes.

332 16 Sept. 1684 John Wootters, Planter, and Martha his wife, to Henry
Aylor, Planter - 100 acres called "Sibland" - adjoining "Pawson's
Ridge" on the west side of Tuckahoe Creek - adjoining the land of Geo.
Bowes. Wit: Richard Dudley, John Davis.

334 10 Sept. 1684 John Wootters and Martha his wife of Tuckahoe, Planter,
to George Bowes, Taylor - 100 acres of 200 on the southeast side - adjoining "Pawson's Ridge" - part of "Sibland." Wit: Richard Dudley,
Benjamin Pride. Bond given by Wootters witnessed by Richard Dudley
and John Davis, 16 Sept. 1684.

335 _____ 1684 Henry Costin of Talbot, Carpenter, to George Burton and
John Shuddall, Planters - 150 acres in Wye River called "Lambeth" -
lying between the heads of Thomas his Branch and Robert Noble's Branch
in the woods - adjoining a marsh on Williams' Branch and land laid out
for George Cowley. Wit: James Cooke, Thomas Emerson, Thomas Collins.

page

337 31 Mar. 1684 John Wootters to John Jadwyne - 250 acres, "Coventry" - at the head of Collbourne's Branch. Wit: John Hall, Thomas Dudley, John Pitts.

338 20 Nov. 1684 Peter Dennis of Talbot, Planter, to Griffith Jones, Gent. - 50 acres on St. Michael's River adjoining the land of Andrew Skinner called "St. Michael's Fresh Runs" - known as "Chance" and adjoining Roger Grosse's "Ashby." Also "Peter's Lott," 50 acres - adjoining "Peter's Chance" adjoining Carter's land on south side St. Michael's River; also a tract adjoining Peter Dennis' plantation and the land of Andrew Skinner. Mentions trees bounded with 16 notches in the presence of William Jump, John Dunne and Timothy Dunnivan. Wit: William Bishopp, Richard Royston, William Presson.

340 20 Oct. 1681 A true account of goods possessed by Peter Dennis within doores and without (Bill of Sale mentioned in above deed):
1 small gelding; 6 cows and calves; 1 3 yr. old heifer; 4 heiffers that will bee 2 about January next; 1 bull, 1 steere, same age.

The goods in the house: 2 featherbeds, 3 bowlsters, 2 pillows, 2 blanketts; 2 ruggs, 1 standing bedstead, 1 trundle bedstead, with cordes to them; 2 chests and 4 chayres; 1 iron pott; 2 gunns; 4 pewter dishes; 4 pewter plates, 1 pewter bason; 2 white juggs with pewter covers to them; 1 podwering tubb; 1 broad axe and 1 hatchet; 1 brass skillet and frame; 1 crosscutt saw; 3 iron potts and 3 payre of potthookes; 1 pewter candlestick, 1 pewter salt; 1 fryeing pan; 1 corn barrell; 1 drawing knife; 1 small table form; 1 payre of bellows; 1 suite of curtains and vallaines; 3 hammers; 2 augurs; 6 napkins; 4 pillow ___ . Now there is several other small things in the house which I shall not mention here butt I have all of them in my booke written downe and as for hogges there is but few for there is but 6 or 7 that is worth anything to increase of. Now for my debts is as followeth: to Richard Sweatnam; Joseph Semphill; Thomas Welsh for wages; Coll. Lloyd; Bryan Omealy; John Perry; Andrew Abbington ___ at Sone's; John Pooley; Thomas Burden; John Bradshaw for work; William Peep for work; Daniel Carnell; William Dixon.

340 20 Jan. 1684 Cornelia Vaughn of Talbot, widdow, to Michael Russell, Planter - 19 acres on west side of Tredhaven Creek near the head - adjoining land formerly Robert Noble's now in possession of Michael Russell. Wit: Philemon Lloyd, James Murphey, George Robotham.

341 14 Nov. 1684 Patrick Ward of Kent County alias St. Joanes, to Henry Wharton of Talbot, Planter - with consent of Elizabeth Ward his wife - 50 acres, a moiety of "Hookland" on north side Choptank River on south side of Second Creek - adjoining land laid out for Andrew Skinner called "Yafford's Neck" - purchased of the said Wharton. Wit: James Murphey, John Kelly. Patrick Ward of Duck Creek, County of Kent alias St. Joanes, to James Murphey of Talbot - P/A. 18 April 1684. Wit: William Mettcalfe, James Doud.

343 23 Dec. 1684 Susannah Cloather, widdow, daughter and heyre of Robert Knapp of Talbot, deceased, to Thomas Impey, Gent. - plantation called

page
"Cromwell" - near the mouth of Harris Creeke at Cromwell's Poynt - 300 acres - mentions Island Creek running into the Chesapeake Bay - also 50 acres adjoining, called "Poplar Necke" now in the tenure of Elizabeth Ward, sometimes the widow and relict of the aforesaid Robert Knapp, deceased. Wit: James Sedgwick, George Impey, Henry Adcock.

345 23 Dec. 1684 Susannah Clothier, widdow, to James Sedgwick, Gent. - P/A. Wit: George Impey, Henry Adcock.

345 29 Dec. 1684 Robert White, Planter, to Robert Devenish of Talbot - 150 acres in Cuthbert's Cove, Harris. Creek, called "Wattson." Wit: Thomas Impey, Edmond Stringer.

346 17 Feb. 1684 John Lane, Planter, to Robert Boreman, Carpenter - 200 acres called "Golden Lyon" - between the northeast branch of Choptank River and Tuckahoe Creek. Wit: Richard White, Edward Turner.

347 17 Feb. 1684 William Purnell, Planter, to Robert Boreman, Carpenter - 200 acres called "Kirkum's Lott" - between the northeast branch of the Choptank and Tuckahoe Creek. Wit: Edward Turner, Richard White.

349 17 Feb. 1684 John Barwicke, Planter, to William Clayton, Planter - 150 acres, part of "Normanton" - adjoining land laid out for William Crosse - near Noble's Branch. Wit: William Finney, Daniel Ingram, William Cross.

351 21 Dec. 1691 Daniel Ingerson of Talbot, Planter, to Henry Snowden, Planter - reference to a contract made between them in 1679 when they became partners. Separation of stocks, both real and personal: Snowden to have "Shoreditch," 150 acres, and all the land in the fork of Williams' Branch commonly called Prosser's Branch, being part of "Wilton," 100 acres - adjoining the land called "Grantum" owned by the partys. The remainder to Daniel Ingerson; he to build Snowden a good, new dwelling on his part of the land, the dimensions to be equal to the new dwelling on the old plantation; a new 40 feet tobacco house and Ingerson to clear for Snowden a parcel amounting to 6000 corn holes and fence the cornfield with a good corn fence 8 railes high and to cleare on the said ground 14,000 tobacco holes with a good worme fence six rayles high and all to be tended 1 year by Daniel Ingerson and then delivered to Snowden and also to make a pasture fence of 3000 rails. Snowden is to have one-half of the fruit of the orchard until his shall beare fruit. Snowden to fall, cut and mall 4000 fence logs for Daniel Ingerson toward ye fencing. Wit: Phillip Hopkins, John Sides, William Hemsley, William Clayton.

Daniel Ingerson's release witnessed 18 Jan. 1691 by John Sides, Thomas Yeowell, Jr. and Henry Pratt.

353 21 Dec. 1691 Henry Snowden to Daniel Ingerson - duplication of the above deed.

TALBOT COUNTY, MARYLAND LAND RECORDS

VOLUME FIVE

page

Pages 001 and 002 are missing in this book; a deed obviously entered on page 002 is continued on page 003.

003 _____ 1684 _____ to William Dixon of Talbot - two tracts of land and a parcel adjoining - all on the eastern branch of St. Michael's River - 50 acres, "Bennett Hill" formerly laid out for John Kinimont, adjoining the land laid out for John and William Shaw, and 150 acres called "Ending of Controversie" on Fausley Branch adjoining the land called "Fausley" laid out for Roger Grosse and the land of Roger Grosse called "Ashby" - and a parcel of 60 acres, part of "Ashby" being a neck of land between Fausley Branch and the eastern branch of the River - on the north side of Fausley Branch - mentions a deed from John Davis to Wenlock Christenson, deceased, father to the wife of the said John Dyne and to her father's will. Wit: Sam. Smith, Edmund Webb. Mary, wife of John Dyne (the grantor) gives her consent.

003 17 Mar. 1684 Francis Bellows to Christopher Santee - 100 acres called "Adventure" on Wye River adjoining Roger Gross' land called "Gross Coate." Wit: Philemon Lloyd, Joseph Hunnywell.

004 15 Mar. 1684 Robert Betts, Planter, to Daniel Baker and Robert Johnson, Planters - 100 acres, part of "Betts' Chance" at the head of Wye River. Wit: Robert Appletree, John Dunn.

004 17 Feb. 1684 William Rich, Planter, and Alice his wife, to Katherine Burgess, wife of John Burgess, Planter - 100 acres, part of "Taylor's Ridge" in the woods on north side Great Choptank River at the head of St. Michael's Creeke. A gift of love to their daughter, Elizabeth Rich, wife of John Blore; both since dead and without issue. John Blore at the time of his death desired the land to be settled on his sister, Katherine, wife of John Burgess, Planter. Wit: Joseph Wollen, Rich. Browne.

006 16 Sept. 1684. James Murphy, Gent., to Thomas Sandiford of Liverpoole, England, Merchant - 100 acres, "Bogshole" on a branch of Second Creek - 100 acres, "Barnes' Neck" and one-half of 100 acres, "Barnes' Neck Addition." Wit: Daniel Carnell, Richard Royston, Griffith Jones.

006 26 May 1684 John Stanley and Christopher Baiteson, Planters, to Thomas Davis, Cooper - 100 acres, one half of a parcel called "Chance" adjoining a dividend sold to Myles Thornton. Wit: Thomas Delehay, Edward Hargreaves. Judith, wife of John Stanley, gives her consent and makes acknowledgment before Edward Man and William Combes. 26 May 1684.

008 6 Jan. 1684 William Rich and Alice his wife, to Francis Harrison, Planter - gift of love to their natural daughter, Mary Harrison - 100 acres, part of "Taylor's Ridge," head of St. Michael's Creek. Wit: T. Delehay, Richard Browne.

page
009 16 June 1685 Sam. Smith of Myles River, Gent., to Edward Stevenson of
     Wye River, Planter - the plantation whereon Stevenson now dwells, 100
     acres called "Atwell Bodell" - also another parcel adjoining, 50 acres
     called "Long Poynte" in Wye River. Wit: Andrew Abbington, Thomas Mount-
     ford.

009 Last day March 1685 James Murphy, Gent., to Daniel Vinton of Talbot,
     Cooper - 150 acres called "Snelling's Delight" - adjoining the land of
     William Godwin on Second Creek. Wit: James Clayland, Lawrence Knowles.

010 1 April 1685 William Jones, Planter, and Sarah his wife, to Ralph Nick-
     son of Talbot - 50 acres, "Jones' Lott" - west side of Harris Creek on
     Phelps' Cove adjoining the land of William Grace and a cove called
     Bridges' Cove. Wit: Vincent Lowe, Henry Parker.

010 26 May 1685 Robert Bishopp of Michaell's River, to my only brother,
     Richard Bishopp, Planter, of Talbot - gift of 200 acres of land in Ches-
     ter River on east side of Langford's Bay, called "Meconikin" - adjoin-
     ing land laid out for Nicholas Broadway. Wit: George Craige, Alexander
     Raye, Ambrose Kinnamont.

011 12 June 1685 Robert Smith of Talbot to Robert Fortune - 150 acres on
     Corsica Creek called "Smith's Reserve" - adjoining the land of Thomas
     Jones called "Pleasant Spring." Wit: Isaac Stone, Robert King.

012 16 June 1685 Peter Sayer, Gent., to Jacob Seth, Planter - 400 acres
     on Wye River called "Mt. Mill." Wit: Thomas Robins, Samuel Smite (Smith).

013 15 May 1685 Richard Holmes, Mary his wife; George Dulin and Martha his
     wife, to Edward Floyd - 100 acres on Myles Creek being a certain part of
     George Watt's land - mentions a division line between Solomon Thomas
     and George Watts. Wit: Joseph Wiggott, John Yate.

014 15 June 1685 John Cornish, Planter, to Thomas Taylor of Dorchsster,
     Planter - 300 acres called "Sutton" - formerly taken up and surveyed for
     George Cowley and conveyed to Richard Cornish the father of John Cor-
     nish - at the head of St. Michael's Creek adjoining the land called
     "Nominy." Wit: T. Delehay, Francis Harrison.

015 1 June 1685 Ann Clymor, widow of John Clymor of Talbot, deceased, to
     Thomas Stevenson - part of a tract at the head of Wye River, taken up
     by Capt. Harwood called "Harwood's Lign" but now called "Stevenson's
     Purchase" - given to Ann Clymor by her former husband and the father of
     the said Thomas Stevenson, viz: Mr. Phillip Stevenson of Talbot, de
     ceased. Wit: Thomas Emerson, William Grosse.

016 14 Nov. 1685 Andrew Skinner, Gent., and Ann his wife to John Cockeral
     of Talbot - 50 acres, "Rodway" between St. Michael's River and Wye Riv-
     er. Wit: George Craige, Richard Hazledine.

016 12 June 1685 Thomas Bruff to Christopher Denny - "Woodland Neck" on
     the south side of Corsica Creek, Talbot County. Wit: Solomon Wright,
     Richard Joanes.

42.

page

018 9 April 1685 Hugh Paxton and Grace his wife, to Jeffrey Mattershaw of Talbot - 100 acres, "Paxton's Lott" adjoining "Butterfield" at the head of Back Wye River - adjoining land of Herbert Craft, Matthew Mason and tract "Green Spring." Wit: Robert Smith, John Purcell.

018 14 Feb. 1685 Robert Smith, Gent., to Nathaniel Tucker, Planter - 200 acres on the south side Chester River called "Jones' his Addition" - adjoining the land in possession of the executor of Thomas Joanes and the land of Richard Tilghman. Wit: Christopher Denny, Richard Higgs, William Powell.

020 18 Aug. 1685 Joseph Billittor, Plasterer, to Thomas Fisher of Talbot, Merchant - 600 acres, "Hackett's Garden" on the east side of Tuckahoe Creek. Wit: Peter Sayer, Griff. Jones, Richard Swettman.

021 2 Aug. 1685 Robert Smith and Ann his wife, to Thomas Collins - part of "Smith's Reserve," 100 acres in Corsica Creek. (no witnesses)

022 25 Apr. 1685 John Vyner of Talbot, Gent., and his wife Elizabeth, to John Eason, Planter - 700 acres formerly called "Claybourne's Island" afterward "Sharp's Island" and now by the name of "Eason's Island." Wit: John Price, John Woodward.

023 11 June 1685 Christopher Baitson, Cooper, and Hannah his wife, to William Welch - 75 acres called "The Wilderness" - adjoining lands of Ralph Dawson, land of Henry Parker called "The Freshes;" and Scott's land called "New Mill." Wit: Jos. Atkins, Samuell Abbott.

025 18 Aug. 1685 Timothy Lane, Planter, to Joseph Billeter, Sr., Plasterer - 100 acres, "Newtowne" on the west side of Tuckahoe Creek adjoining the land laid out for William Berry. Wit: James Sylvester, Daniel Morrihy.

025 14 Aug. 1685 Robert Smith and Ann his wife, to Isaac Stone of Talbot - 200 acres in the branches of Corsica Creek - adjoining land laid out for Steven Tully in possession of William Cowell. Wit: Richard Mackline, Thomas Bruff.

026 10 Sept. 1685 John Robinson and Ann his wife, Planter, to John Gaterly of Talbot, Planter - 200 acres, "Chestnut Meadow" - on Tuckahoe Creek adjoining a tract called "Providence" formerly laid out for Stephen Tully and the said John Robinson. Wit: John Hawkins, John Edmondson, James Clarke. Anny Robinson to Richard Sweatman - P/A. Wit: Walter Talbott, William Bennett.

028 15 Sept. 1685 James Smith of Talbot, Planter to William Bush, Planter - 200 acres, part of "Smith's Land" on the branches of Double Creek in Chester River. Wit: Henry Parker, Richard Jones, Sr.

029 12 Sept. 1685 Robert Ellis and Gartery his wife, to Andrew Furby - 100 acres on Corsica Creek - part of "Rexam Plaines." Wit: Richard Jones, John Robertson, John Thomson.

page
029 28 Aug. 1685 Robert Northest of Talbot, Carpenter, and Tabitha his
     wife, to Thomas Punney, Carpenter - 2 tracts at the head of Corsica Cr.
     and Matthais' Branch, called "Claxon Hill" and "Jones' Forrest."
     Wit: William Hemsley, Thomas Collins.

030 (no date) Michael Miller of Kent and Ann his wife, to Thomas Jackson,
     Planter - 125 acres called "Winchester" in Talbot County in Winchester
     Creek, south side Chsster River. Wit: Albert Blocke, Sarah Hunter.
     Letter to William Harris of Kent County giving P/A, witnessed by Thomas
     Joce and Robert Smith. Elias King, Planter, of Kent, wit. to William
     Harris' letter.

031 15 Sept. 1685 John Edmondson, Merchant, to Edmond Fish, Planter - in
     consideration of one bay horse and 1200 lbs. of tobacco - 100 acres
     called "Batchelor's Range Addition" near branch of King's Creek called
     Wottenhawke's Branch" - partly within the bounds of "Mt. Hope." Wit:
     John Hawkins, Abraham Morgan, Sam. Smith.

032 3 Oct. 1681 William Milton to brother Roger Milton of New Jersey,
     Delaware River in America - moiety in a plantation in Chester River,
     Talbot County. Wit: Wm. Steere, William Ford, Elezar Hooke.

     9 Mar. 1679 William Milton of Salem, Delaware River, New Jersey, Tallow
     Chandler, fr. John Hussey of Shottsbrooke, Co. Berkshire, England, shoe-
     maker - refer to deed by John Hussey and Mary his wife to William Mil-
     ton - a plantation of 200 acres willed by John Singleton, deceased, to
     Mary Hawden, now wife of John Hussey - now in the occupation of Henry
     Willcockes and Charles Hollingsworth. Wit: Stephen Edwards, Robert
     Boult, William Hearne. Henry Willcockes and Charles Hollingsworth men-
     tioned as overseers of Singleton's will. Sealed and delivered before
     William Steere and Eleazor Hooke of Workingham, County of Berks, Eng.,
     Notary, and William Ford. 3 Oct. 1681

034 19 June 1685 Roger Milton of Windham Farm, Salem, New West Jersey, to
     William Boulton of Chester River, Planter - "Refers to John Singleton's
     will devising to Mary Hawden now wife of John Hussey of Shotsbrooke in
     County Berkshire, Kingdome of England, Cordwainer - a moyety of a plan-
     tation in Chester River; and John Hussey and Mary his wife on 9 March
     1679 sold to William Milton late of Salem on Delaware River in the Prov-
     ince of West Jersey, Tallow Chandler. William Milton sold it to his
     brother Roger Milton of Windam, West Jersey" - in consideration of the
     sum of L55 paid by William Boulton of Chester River; Milton conveys
     a moiety or half part of the aforesaid plantation. 2 Oct. 1684.
     Charles Hollingsworth from Roger Milton, P/A, wit. by William Hollings-
     worth, Edward French. Roger Rydwood, James Nevill, wit. to deed.

035 17 Nov. 1685 John Brewer of Ann Arundell Co. and Sarah his wife, to
     Thomas Emerson, Gent. - 320 acres called "Widdow's Chance" at the head
     of Wye River - adjoining land of John Davis. Wit: Will. Hemsley, John
     Emerson.

035 17 Nov. 1685 John Brewer of Ann Arundell and Sarah his wife, to John
     Davis of Talbot, Gent. - 320 acres, half part of "Widdow's Chance" on

page

south side Cabin Run. Wit: Wm. Hemsley, John Emerson.

036 19 Sept. 1685 Peter Dodd to Elizabeth Chance - Marriage Contract -
mentions her sons William and Richard Chance - mentions Betty's Cove
Meetinghouse. Wit: Walter Lister, Philemon Armstrong.

038 17 Nov. 1685 William Younge, Planter, and Frances his wife, to Symon
Harris - 175 acres called "Young's Adventure" on Thomas' Branch of Wye
River - adjoining "Ditteridge" formerly laid out for Richard Bridges;
and "Prouse's Park." Wit: Andrew Abington, Thomas Emerson, William
Cleton.

038 6 Nov. 1685 Francis Sheppheard of Talbot and Hannah his wife, to Thom-
as Collins - 200 acres called "Ashford" on the south side Chester River,
Talbot County - adjoining the land laid out for Francis Sheppheard and
William Tillghman - mention land called "Hemingfield." Wit: J. Sempill,
R. Goldsborough.

039 18 Aug. 1685 Richard Jones, Jr., Planter, to Robert Norrest, Planter -
200 acres, "Jones' Parke" on south side Chester River, north side Cor-
sicall Creek - lease. Wit: John Lillingston, William Tonge.

040 1 Dec. 1685 Richard Hazledine, Planter, and Abigail his wife, to Henrietta Maria Lloyd, relict to Col. Philemon Lloyd - 50 acres, "Town Road"
on the east side St. Michael's River, north side Champ's Creek. Wit:
Michael Turbutt, John Davis.

041 20 Jan. 1685 Robert Hawkshaw of Talbot and Margaret his wife, by their
attorney, Robert Smith, to Thomas Harmon, Merchant, of London, England -
200 acres, "Parker's Lott" on the southeast branch of Chester River.
Wit: Henry Green, Thomas Collins. Margaret Hawkshaw's P/A witnessed by
George Hasfurt and Henry Everett.

041 21 Dec. 1685 Thomas Willson of St. Joanes, to Thomas Smith of Talbot -
150 acres called "Lamberton" on Anderby's Creek in Choptank River.
Wit: Thomas Hopkins, Jr., Benjamin Pecke. Robert Tow, Atty. for Thomas
Willson.

042 14 Jan. 1685 Henry Pratt, Planter, and Seth his wife, to John Morgan,
Planter - 100 acres, part of "Willton" on Williams' Branch of Wye River -
mentions Edward Barrowclift's millpond. Wit: John Sargent, Phillip
Hopkins.

043 19 Jan. 1685 Robert Betts, Planter, to James Smith of Talbot, Carpenter -
100 acres on north side Choptank River, head of Tuckahoe Creek, Frenchwoman's Branch - called "Tattnell." Wit: Michael Hackett, John Gardner.

044 15 Jan. 1685 Simon Wilmer and Rebecca his wife, by their attorney
Francis Shepheard, to Thomas and Richard Eubancks of Talbot - 300 acres,
one-half of "Poplar Hill" in Chester River. Wit: Thomas Seaward,
Claudius Dutitre.

page
045 15 Jan. 1685 Simon Wilmer and Rebecca his wife, by their attorney
Francis Shepheard, to Jonas Greenwood of Talbot - one-half of "Poplar
Hill" in Fishing Creek, Chester River. Wit: Thomas Seaward, Claudius
Dutitre. Bond given to Greenwood witnessed by Richard Sweatnam and
Richard Jones.

047 14 Jan. 1685 Francis Shepheard, Planter, to William Britton of Bithe-
ford, Old England, Mariner - "Barfield" and "Heminfield" on Jones' Creek
alias Brittland Creek, Chester River. Wit: Robert Smith, Thomas Thomas,
Matthew Tomlins.

048 16 Jan. 1685 Henry Costine, Planter, to Henrietta Maria Lloyd, relict
of Col. Philemon Lloyd - 500 acres, his part of "Lloyd's Costin" on
Williams' Branch of Wye River. Wit: Richard Wynne, Joseph Hunnywell,
Richard Bennett.

049 6 Nov. 1685 John Boone of Talbot, Planter, to Edward Starke - one-
half of "Boon's Hope" at the head of the Choptank River. Wit: John
Seaton, Nicholas Banks.

049 10 Aug. 1685 James Peacocke, Stockton upon Tease, County and Bishoprick of Durham, England, Master and Mariner, to Thomas Cooke and Hester
his wife, of the same place, Shipwright - one-half part of 500 acres
called "Parker's Park" in King's Creek, Choptank River. Granted to
Henry Parker of Dorchester County, sold to William Southbe, who on 8
April 1684 conveyed to Peacocke - mentions the watermill. Wit: Richard
Wattson, William Dodgworth, Robert Grundy, Thos. Attkinson.

051 14 Mar. 1685 Robert Betts to Oliver Milliton - 100 acres, part of
"Betts' Chance" on Tuckahoe Creek, Choptank River - adjoining the part
sold by Betts to Robert Johnson and Daniell Baker.   Also "Betts'
Addition" adjoining "Betts' Chance" and "Easome." (no witnesses)

052 26 Jan. 1685 Henry Parker, Gent., to Andrew Abington - 400 acres,
"Warwicke," in a fork of King's Creek between Woodenhawk's Branch and
Hapnabb's Branch - adjoining "The Square" laid out for John Edmondson
and Joseph Sone; "Chancellor's Mannor" and 'The Adventure.' Wit:
Richard Swann, Elinor Dudley.

053 15 Jan. 1686 Judith Hemsley, widow, to her son Charles Hemsley -
200 acres, "Newarke Upon Trent" - mentions Island Point. Wit: James
Davis, Mary Thrift, Michael Earle.

053 8 Feb. 1685 Thomas Games, Sr., Planter, and Martha his wife, to James
Bampton, Blacksmith - land purchased from Edward Roe, late of Talbot,
Gent., 100 acres called "Chance" - granted to George Langford for 150
acres - on Island Creek out of Choptank River - adjoining the land of
Francis Parrott laid out for Andrew Skinner; adjoining the land of
Robert Curtis and the land "Anderton." Wit: Jos. Atkins, Alex. Wilson.

055 15 June 1686 John Hollingsworth and Jane his wife, to Wm. Hemsley -
300 acres called "Jerusalem" on south side Chester River. Wit: Jos.
Atkins, Robert Ellis.

page

055 12 April 1686 John Eason of Talbot, Planter, son and heir of John
Eason, Planter, deceased, and Mary his wife, to John Viner, Gent. -
in exchange for 1000 acres called "Wolsley Mannor" - 700 acres, "Cla-
bourne's Island" lately "Sharp's Island" - formerly in the tenure of
John Bateman, deceased, and by Bateman and Mary his wife, sold to Peter
Sharpe, Chyrurgion, and by William Sharp (son and heir of Peter Sharp)
and Elizabeth his wife to John Eason father of the grantor. Wit: Robt.
Goldsborough, T. Delehay, John Woodward.

056 15 June 1686 Nicholas Hackett, Planter, to Richard Sweatnam of Talbot,
Innholder - 250 acres called "Hackton" - adjoining land laid out for
William Berry on Tuckahoe Creek, out of Choptank River. Wit: Henry
Parker, Thomas Anderson.

056 16 Feb. 1686 Michaell Hackett and Mary his wife, to Robert Hawkshaw,
Planter - 200 acres, "Bradford" and "Bradford's Addition." Wit: George
Gorsuch, Edward Elliott.

057 15 June 1686 William Berry, Sr. and Margarett his wife, to Margarett
Pinner, widow - 130 acres called "Berry's Range" near the nouth of High-
field Creek, Tuckahoe, and adjoining "Highfield's Addition." Wit: John
Alexander, John Lane.

058 7 April 1686 Mary Mecotter, relict of Alexander Mecotter of Talbot,
Planter, deceased, from her son Alexander Mecotter and Ann his wife -
"Sutton's Grange" on Bullenbrook Creek out of Choptank River. Wit:
Daniel Carnell, John Stanley, R. Gouldsborough.

058 31 Oct. 1685 John Greene of Ann Arundell Co., Planter, to Francis and
John Watts, sons of Francis Watts of Ann Arundell, deceased - land granted to William Snaggs and by him to Richard Snowden of Road River and by
Snowden to Greene - "Batchelor's Delight" - 100 acres on Wye River -
adjoining the land laid out for John Wright, Merchant, and the land laid
out for William Smith. Wit: Thomas Taylor, Wm. Burgess, Henry Hanslap.
P/A to William Grosse witnessed by William Hambleton and Hester Grosse.

060 28 Apr. 1686 George Robins, Gent. and Margarett his wife, to Timothy
Lane of Talbot, Planter - 500 acres called "Lambert" on north side of
Choptank River and Tuckahoe Creek - adjoining the land of William Kirk-
ham. Wit: John Stanley, William Bexley, John Mann.

061 16 Mar. 1685 William Hemsley of Talbot, Gent., and Cornelia his wife,
to Richard Sweatnam, Gent. - 900 acres called "Chesterfield" on Coursica
Creek in Chester River. Wit: Griffith Jones, Tho. Vaughn, Mich. Earll.

063 6 Aug. 1686 John Harwood, Planter, to William Browne, Planter - 200
acres, part of "Ritch Farm" on the branches of King's Creek - originally
400 acres - adjoining 100 acres sold by Harwood to John Dyne and the
land of John Pitts. Wit: Thos. Loggins, John Burton, R. Gouldsborough.

064 16 Aug. 1686 Robert Smith, Gent., and Ann his wife, to John Symons,
Planter - 100 acres, one-half of "Smithfield" - adjoining the land of

page
    John Robinson. Wit: Thomas Bruff, John Wrightson.

065 17 Aug. 1686 William Dixon of Miles River, Gent., and Elizabeth his wife, to Samuel Wosle and George Palmer of King's Creek, Planters - 100 acres called "Dixon's Lott" in King's Creek adjoining the land of Richard Harwood, called "Rich Farme" on the west side of Chancellor's Branch. Wit: Walter Lister, William Browne.

065 11 Aug. 1686 Michael Hackett to Robert Smith - 250 acres, "Hackett's Chance" in Singleton's Neck, Chester River in Talbot County. Wit: Simon Willmour, Will. Hemsley.

066 11 Aug. 1686 John Bayly of Talbot, Planter, to Daniell Carnell, Gent. - 100 acres on east side Tredhaven Creek on Taylor's Branch - adjoining the land of William Turner - mentions "Graves' Point" - also "Bayly's Lott" on Parrott's Branch of Thirdhaven Creek adjoining "Turner's Point" - 135 acres. Wit: William Dixon, Samuel Withers, Griff. Jones.

067 5 Feb. 1686 Christopher Baitson and Hannah his wife, to William Anderson of Talbot - 124 acres called "Prospect" on the north side of St. Michael's Creek adjoining the land of Robert Knapp. Wit: Jos. Atkins, Samuell Abbott, James Colland.

067 17 Aug. 1686 William Hemsley and Judith Hemsley his mother, widow, to my two brothers Charles and Philemon - 200 acres in the occupation of our mother - laid out for one Cary of London, Merchant, in Wye River on Wye Island -(division given) - brothers above to purchase from our brother Vincent. Wit: Joseph Emerson, Michael Earle.

068 12 June 1686 Thomas Croft to George Phillips, both of Talbot - 80 acres called "Spring Branch" on the west side of Wickamis Branch - described in a deed from Richard Jones, Sr. to Thomas Croft. Wit: Robert Smith, Daniell Glover, Zacharias Thompson, Wm. Gibson, Wm. Hardes, Rich. Jones.

069 16 Aug. 1686 Robert Ellis, Plaisterer, to Robert Smith, Gent. - 365 acres called "Wrexam's Plains" - excepting 100 acres sold to Andrew Currey. Wit: John Londey, Daniell Carnell.

069 10 Jan. 1686 Vincent Lowe of Great Choptank Island to Elizabeth Oakley of Talbot, widdow - 2 parcels, 150 acres, "Merchant's Folly" - near "Myles End" laid out for Thomas Myles - also 150 acres, "Rich Neck" near to the land of Thomas Vaughn called "Merchant's Folly" - mentions Cabbin Cove, Harris Creek. Wit: Nicholas Lowe, Thomas Vaughn.

070 20 Sept. 1686 Richard Dudley, Taylor, and Elinor his wife, to Thomas Allcocke, Weaver - 100 acres, the southern part of "Dudley's Choice" on west side of Tuckahoe Creek - back of the land laid out for John Pawson - mentions Haman's Branch and land called "Dudley." Wit: Edmond Gary, Thomas Jackson, Daniell Carnell.

071 16 Nov. 1686 Alice Kirkham, widdow, to William Jones, Planter - 150 acres called "Mt. Hope" on the west side of Choptank River. Wit: Thos. Blackburne, George Hurlocke.

page

071   19 Oct. 1686   Richard Dudley and Ellinor his wife, to Anthony Phillips, Planter - 200 acres, "Dudley's Desire" on the east side of Tuckahoe Creek - adjoining land laid out for William Jump - surveyed 1682.
Wit: William Berry, Jr., John Bonnwell.

072   16 Nov. 1686   Alice Kirkham to William Jones - Bond. Wit: Thomas Black-
burn, George Hurlocke, Matthew Jenkins.

072   14 Aug. 1686   John Edmondson, Merchant, and Sarah his wife, to William
Caltrop, Planter - 200 acres, part of "Mt. Hope" (containing in the whole
700 acres) - adjoining 100 acres of the same belonging to Edmond Fish.
Wit: John Lane, Will. Rodeney, Thos. Smithson, James Benson, Major Peter
Sayer. Bond witnessed by Simon Willmer, Jona. Craycroft.

073   30 Dec. 1686   Abraham Morgan and Elizabeth his wife, to Walter Quinton =
150 acres, part of 400 acres called "Gouldesbrough" in Tredhaven Creek,
on Bullenbrooke Road. Wit: Michael Turbutt, Nicholas Lowe.

074   13 Sept. 1686   Ellinor Bradbury of Talbot, widow, to Thomas Alcocke -
100 acres west side Tuckahoe Creek, late the property of John Spooner
who by his last will and testament devised to Ellinor Bradbury - Ann
Spooner, his widow, holds a life interest. Wit: Michaell Meginney,
Edward Butler.

074   22 Apr. 1686   William Belchier of London, England, Merchant, to Myles
Hatton of London, Merchant, now residing in Maryland - P/A. Wit:
Elizabeth Garnis, John Woodward, Edward Mann.

075   19 Jan. 1686   Benjamin Pride and Jane his wife, to John Johnson - 100
acres on Hambleton's Branch in Chester River - part of "Ripley," laid
out for Stephen Tully for 950 acres. Wit: Will. Coursey, Simon Willmer.

076   17 Jan. 1686   John Eason of Talbot, Planter, and Mary his wife, to Clement Sale, Planter - 1000 acres, the "Mannour of Woolsey" - on the north
side of Great Choptank River - begins at a marked oak upon a poynt by
a marsh respecting an Indian town to the southeast - conveyed by Philip
Calvert, deceased, to Richard Preston, Sr. of Calvert County and by him
to Henry Stracy a London merchant; and by him to William Vyner of Salls-
bury, County of Wells___, Alderman and by him to John Viner son and heir
of the said William and by Viner to John Eason. Originally patented
18 Jan. 1659. Wit: John Nedith, John Woodward.

077   20 Jan. 1686   Edward Kitchener, Planter, to John Power, Planter - 50
acres, "Freeman's Rest" in Second Creek - adjoining James Olliver -
formerly laid out for Timothy Freeman, deceased. Wit: Vincent Lowe,
Andrew Sexton.

077   17 Jan. 1686   George Aldridg, Carpenter, to John Aldridg, Planter -
one-half of "Indian Necke" - 350 acres near Talbot County Courthouse,
Wye River. Wit: Wm. Hemsley.

078   17 Jan. 1686   John Aldridg to his brother Thomas, a minor. Bond guar-

49.

anteeing transfer of the above land - one-half of 175 acres. Wit: Wm.
Hemsley, Michael Earle.

078 15 Nov. 1686 Michael Hackett and Mary his wife, to Daniel Dempsey -
100 acres called "Highgate Lane" on south side Chester River, south side
of the eastern branch - adjoining the land laid out for Henry Parker -
"Parker's Lott." Wit: Elizabeth Laula, George Hasfurt. Mary Hackett to
Robert Smith - P/A, witnessed by Geo. Hasfurt and Richard Collins.

080 3 Nov. 1686 Andrew Skinner, Gent. to John King, Planter, my only son-
in-law - gift of 320 acres on Turkey Creek, called "Rocliffe." Wit:
George Craige, Robert Baites, John Jones.

23 Aug. 1686 Andrew Skinner, Gent., to my eldest daughter Elizabeth,
wife of John King, Planter - 120 acres called "Timbernecke" - lying
towards the head of Michaell's River. Wit: George Craige, Richard Skinner, Thomas Gibson.

080 14 Feb. 1686 Benjamin Pecke to John Games - 75 acres, part of "Hopkins
Point" on the western side of Tredhaven Creek - adjoining the now dwelling house of John Games and adjoining the land of Thomas Hopkins. Wit:
R. Gouldesborough, George Hurlocke. Vincent Lowe to John Games - a
receipt for one shilling, alienation fee.

081 2 Mar. 1686 Henrietta Maria Lloyd of Talbot from James Scott, Planter,
and Margarett, his wife - "Timberland" on the west side of Tuckahoe Cr.,
on northwest side of "Lloyd's Parke," formerly laid out for Coll. Phil.
Lloyd - adjoining "Sallisberry Plaine" - according to patent, granted
13 Nov. 1683, 400 acres. Wit: Richard Skinner, Richard Wynne, Archbold
Johnson. Margarett Scott to Richard Wynne - P/A to acknowledge the deed
and surrender her right of dower, 15 Mar. 1686. Wit: Richard Skinner,
Elizabeth King.

082 17 Aug. 1686 James Scott, Planter, to Robert Smith, Gent. - 150 acres,
"Scott's Lott" - lately belonging to James Scott, his father, and now in
his possession - the south side of Coursegall Creek in Talbot County.
Adjoining the land of Alexander Maxwell. Wit: Thos. Emerson, John Thrift.

082 5 Aug. 1686 Samuel Withers of Ann Arundell County, Gent., to Richard
Hill of Ann Arundell, Gent. - 600 acres, "Suffolk" in Talbot, north side
of Choptank River in Tuckahoe Creek - 600 acres. Wit: William Walker,
George Bird. Peter Sayer, Sheriff, to Capt. Richard Hill - receipt for
12 shillings sterling, alienation money.

083 10 Mar. 1686 Nathaniel Wright of Chester River, to Nathaniel Tucker -
100 acres, "Adventure" on south side Chester River - adjoining "Jones'
Addition," formerly laid out for Thomas Jones. Wit: Wm. Coursey, Thos.
Thomas.

085 19 Feb. 1686 Robert Clarke, Planter, to Robert Hardinge, Planter - one-
fourth part of one-half part of land on northeast side Choptank River,
patent granted to Edward Lloyd, Gent., 10 Jan. 1659 - adjoining land sold
by Edw. Lloyd to John Boone, and "The Wilderness," comprising 600 acres.

page

the lower half lately possessed by Richard Moore and William Prisk - adjoining the land of Joseph James, Francis Harrison. Wit: Edward Mann and William Combes.

086 19 Feb. 1686 Robert Clarke, Planter, to Francis Harrison, Planter - one-fourth of one-half of the above - his quarter on Island Creek, Choptank River, adjoining the plantation of Thomas Bowdell. Wit: William Combes, Edward Mann.

087 25 Sept. 1686 Coll. William Coulebourne of Somerset County, Gent., to John Wootters of Talbot, Planter - 2000 acres called "Smith's Cliffts" in Tuckahoe Creek on the western side - adjoining the land of Peter Sharpe - mentions a marked beach tree standing on a poynt of an Indian field. Wit: Thos. Newbold, Edmond Howard. Acknowledged before Coll. William Stevens and Thomas Newbold, Justices. Peter Sayer, Sheriff, to John Wootters - receipt for eight shillings - alienation fee.

087 30 May 1687 Ann Moody of Talbot, Spinster, to William Dickinson, Planter - indenture of her son Palmerin Moody to serve as an apprentice until he is thirty (sic) and one years. Dickinson agrees to find all things necessary and fitting for an apprentice of his rank and to teach him to read, write and cost account. Wit: John Preston, Thomas Delehay.

087 21 June 1687 Francis Shepard, Planter, and Hannah his wife, to Frances Mitchell, daughter to John Michaell, deceased - all that messuage or tenement called "Shaver" in Talbot, on the south side Chester River on Unicorn Branch - adjoining 1000 acres in possession of Simon Wilmore - laid out for 200 acres. Wit: Wm. Hemsley, William Scott.

088 9 Mar. 1687 John Lillingston, Clk., and Simon Willmer, Gent., to George Powell, Planter - bond guaranteeing deed made by Mary Tilghman, widow, to George Powell for part of land called "Partnership" - mentions Richard Tilghman, son of Mary Tilghman. Wit: William Tonge, Richard Tilghman.

088 11 June 1687 Arthur Charleton of Cecil County, Gent., to John Wootters - P/A. Wit: Henry Ealor, Thomas Bradshaw, Susanna Daniell.

089 17 June 1687 Arthur Carleton, Sr., of Cecil County, to John Richards of Talbot, Carpenter - 400 acres called "Millford" on the east side of Tuckahoe Creek on a creek called Millford Haven - formerly belonging to John Morgan late of Talbot, deceased, who by his will 23 Feb. 1675 bequeathed to Elizabeth his wife, who afterwards intermarried with Arthur Carleton and had issue by her one daughter which said Elizabeth deceasing bequeathed the same to the said Arthur Carleton her husband. Wit: Martin Hoogland, Will. Arny.

089 ____ June 1687 John Price, Brickmaker, to John Porter, Planter - part of 100 acres known as "Mt. Misery" on Second Creek - first purchased of Thomas Hethod and of him by James Murphy and of him by William Bell and of Bell by Lawrence Porter and of him by John Price. Wit: Henry Adcocke, Hugh Sherwood.

page

090 28 Sept. 1686 William Hill to William Darvall of Kent, Province of
Pensillvania - "Hill's Addition" on the east side of Tuckahoe Creek -
adjoining Nicholas Hackett, John Morgan and Morgan's Creek - surveyed
8 Sept. 1679 for 50 acres. Wit: Thomas Jeoffres, Elizabeth Welch, Wm.
Bourne. Acknowledged by William Hill, 14 Feb. 1686/7 before William
Clark, William Willson and William Lawrence, Justices of Kent County.
William Rodney, Clerk.

090 28 Sept. 1686 William Hill, Sr., Planter, to William Durvall of Kent
County, Province of Penna. - 450 acres called "Hackfield" on Tuckahoe
Creek - adjoining Morgan's Creek and Hackfield Creek. Wit: Thomas
Jeoffres, Elizabeth Wallis, William Bowen. Acknowledged before the
Justices abovementioned.

091 28 Sept. 1686 William Hill, Sr. to John Edmondson, John Baynard and/or
Richard Dudley - P/A - in Dover River, Kent County, Delaware Bay, Territory of Penn. Wit: Thos. Jeoffres, Elizabeth Wallis, William Born.

091 21 June 1687 John Miles of Ann Arundell County, Planter, to Daniel
Walker of Talbot, Planter - 50 acres formerly laid out for Thomas Miles
of Ann Arundell, deceased, called "Miles' Fifty Acres" - also 50 acres
called "Millington" in St. Michael's River, on Ashby Branch. Wit:
Michael Russell, Abraham Hurlock.

091 9 Mar. 1686 Francis Shepheard to George Powell - release of claim to
the land "Partnership" - patented 1 Oct. 1682 to him and William Tilghman and divided during the time of William Tilghman and sold by Mary
Tilghman, widow, to George Powell.

9 Mar. 1686 Mary Tilghman, widow, to George Powell - 250 acres, part
of "Partnership" in Talbot County on the south side of Chester River
in the woods - back of land laid out for Richard Royston called "Royston's." Patented to William Tilghman and Francis Shepheard, 1 Oct.
1682. Wit: William Tonge, Richard Tilghman.

092 26 Aug. 1687 Thomas Bruff of Chester River, Talbot County, to Edward
Stevenson - 400 acres called "Sailsbury Plaine" - near Tuckahoe Creek -
part of a warrant granted to Timothy Goodridge and assigned to John
Richardson of Talbot 27 Nov. 1670 - and by Richardson to Edward Will-
iams and by Williams to Robert Turner and by Turner or his assigns to
John Stanley and by him to Thomas Hutchinson and by him to Thomas Bruff.
Adjoining the land of John Edmondson and the land of Col. Philemon
Lloyd. Wit: Henry Lognes, Anna Denny, Sarah Earle, Mich. Earle.

093 1 June 1687 John Kinnimont of St. Michael's River, Planter, to his son,
Ambrose Kinnimont, Planter - 100 acres, "Fentry" - north side Hunting
Creek - adjoining the land formerly laid out for Edmond Webb called
"Edmonton" - patented 6 Aug. 1664. Wit: James Scott, Thomas Emerson,
Michael Earle.

093 1 Sept. 1687 Richard Burkett, Planter, to Thomas Collins - 100 acres,
part of "Spread Eagle," southeast branch of Chester River adjoining the
land of John Offley. Wit: James Smith, Leonard Coxson.

093   18 June 1687 Robert Smith to John Jones, Brazier - 300 acres, "Triangle's Addition" - adjoining "Triangle," laid out for Robert Smith -
adjoining the land of George Pascall; Jonathon Sibery, Richard Jones
and Matthais Peterson. The tract is on a branch of Henry Green's Cove,
in the woods. Wit: John Lovett, Philip Davis.

094   20 June 1687 Robert Kent to Robert Smith - 100 acres, part of "Neglect" on Reed's Creek and Wells' Poynt. Wit: Thomas Vaughn, Thomas
Bruff.

095   21 Aug. 1683 John Lane, Planter, and Mary his wife, to Joseph Hicks -
150 acres, "Charlville" near a branch of Tuckahoe Creek - patented 25
January 1681. Wit: Thomas Delehay, Daniel Carnell.

096   20 June 1687 Thomas Adkock and Elizabeth his wife, to John Kelld -
100 acres called "Allcock's Addition" adjoining a tract called "Part-
nershipp" on Tuckahoe Creek - intersecting with the land of Thomas
Austin - patented 3 Aug. 1682. Wit: John Thrift, Joseph West.

097   27 May 1687 John Edmondson and Sarah his wife, to William Ridgaway,
Planter - 140 acres called "Westland," north side Great Choptank River near Benoni's Poynt at the mouth of Tredhaven Creek - mentions the
thoroughfare that comes out of Choptank River into Thirdhaven - towards
the northwest up Foxhole Creek - adjoined on the north by the land of
William Harris and Joseph Rogers. Wit: Abraham Morgan, Joseph Scott.

098   27 May 1687 William Ridgway and Alice his wife, to Joseph Rogers -
20 acres, part of "Westland" - surveyed and laid out for John Edmondson. Wit: Henry Adcock, Erick Imbritson. Received of Thomas Booker
for Joseph Rogers, 9 pence 3 farthings, alienation fee. Nicholas Lowe.

099   25 May 1687 Joseph Hicks, Planter, to Nicholas Northover, Planter -
150 acres, "Charlville" - near a branch of Tuckahoe Creek. Wit: Thos.
Loggins, James Smith.

100   (no date) 1687 Joseph Hicks to Nicholas Northover - 100 acres called
"Corke" - adjoining "Charlville" near Tuckahoe Creek - patented to John
Lane. Wit: Thomas Loggins, James Smith.

100   20 June 1687 William Rodgers and Dorothy his wife, to John Pearle -
100 acres, the southwest end of a parcel of land adjoining the land
called "Prophecy" on the southwest branch of Island Creek, Chester River - formerly laid out for Daniel Jenifer for 500 acres. Wit: Francis
Hollingsworth, Jonas Greenwood.

102   15 Dec. 1686 James Clayland to John King - 100 acres, "Parsonage Addition" - north side St. Michael's River near Camp's Creek - adjoining
the land laid out for Andrew Skinner called "Forke Necke" and land
called "Tanner's Help." Wit: George Craig, John Ross, Elizabeth Clayland.

103 16 Aug. 1687 John Salter, Joyner, of Kent County, and Mary his wife,
to Robert Grundy of Yarn, County of York in old England, Merchant -
200 acres called "Plain Dealing" on north side Choptank River, western
branch of Tredhaven Creek and in a small branch called the Halling
Branch - and 50 acres on the eastern side of "Plain Dealing" called
"Wyatt's Fortune." Wit: Edward Pollard, Elias King.

104 16 Aug. 1687 Thomas Hutchinson of Threadhaven, Tanner, to Thomas Bruff,
Gent. - 400 acres, "Salisbury Plain" - part of a warrant for 1700 acres
granted to Timothy Goodridge of Talbot, 24 Nov. 1670. Goodridge
assigned to John Richardson (reference to patent 10 July 1671); Richardson to Edward Williams; Williams to Robert Turner and Turner's
assigns to John Stanley and by Stanley to Hutchinson - adjoining John
Edmondson and Philemon Lloyd. Wit: Philemon Hemsley, William Cathrupp,
Richard Swettnam.

105 16 Aug. 1687 Collonel Vincent Lowe, Esq., to John Tyly, Planter -
143 acres, "Hackett's Field" - adjoining the land lately in possession
of John Viner. Wit: John Lane, Samuel Smith.

106 6 June 1687 Francis Armstrong, Planter, to Thomas Booker - 50 acres
part of "Tilghman's Fortune" at the head of a branch of Tredhaven Creek
adjoining the land of Egbert Garrison and the land of Capt. Robert Morris. Wit: Henry Adcock, Daniel Carnell.

107 24 Jan. 1688 Acknowledged before Edward Man and George Robins, Justices.
Received of Thomas Booker 1 shilling alienation fee. Nicholas Lowe.

107 16 Aug. 1687 John Edmondson, Merchant, and Sarah his wife, to Vincent
Lowe, Esq. - 1000 acres called "The Four Square" at the head of King's
Creek - the beginning at the Chancellor's tree. Wit: Thomas Delehay,
Francis Harrison. Sarah Edmondson to Thomas Delehay - P/A witnessed
by Francis Harrison and Edward Jones.

107 16 Sug. 1687 Coll. V. Lowe, Esq., to Samuel Taylor - 1000 acres called
"Low's Arcadia" - south side Chester River on Island Creek - adjoining
land laid out for Andrew Price called "Good Increase." Wit: James Murphy, Daniel Carnell.

108 15 Aug. 1687 Coll. Vincent Lowe, Esq., to Rice Evans, Planter - 50
acres of land on the east side of Choptank (sic) Bay in Talbot County -
formerly laid out for Samuel Hall - part of Harris' Mannor - on Cabbin
Creek adjoining the land of James Rigby. Also a parcel of 50 acres respecting the plantation of Robert Lambdin, part of Harris' Mannour and
part of a tract commonly called "Goose Neck" on Harris' Creek. The first
50 acres now in the tenure of William Grace. Wit: James Murphey, Geo.
Robotham.

109 (no date) Thomas Wetherby, House Carpenter, to George Paulus Vander-
ford of Talbot - one-half of "Ashton" on the south side Chester River
in Hambleton's Creek - the upper eastern part - adjoining the land laid
out formerly for Stephen Tully - first taken by Stephen Tully and sold

to John Breame and by him to Wetherby. Wit: John Whittington, James Smith.

111 16 Aug. 1687 John Newnam, Planter, and Mary his wife, to John Davis, Planter - consideration of payment of 5500 lbs of tobacco to Newnam and of five shillings to Mary his wife - 200 acres called "Bedworth" on the east side of Woodenhawk Branch, King's Creek - adjoining land laid out for Robert Norwood and "The Square" laid out for John Edmondson and Joseph Soane. Wit: Wm. Finney, Daniel Walker.

112 18 June 1687 Joseph Wickes and John Hynson of Kent County to John Chiers of Talbot, Cooper - 450 acres called "Lently" in a fresh run of Corsica Creek, south side Chester River about two miles from the creekside. Wit: John Davis, Claudius Dutitre.

112 _____ 1687 Johana Whittington to James Smith - P/A. Wit: Edward Plesto, John _____ .

113 11 Sept. 1687 John Whittington and Johana his wife, to John Hoult - 100 acres, the upper part, a moiety of "Whittington's Lott" in Chester River - adjoining the plantation where John Whittington now lives. Wit: Joseph Cudworth, John Jacob.

115 16 Aug. 1687 Richard Beck and Mary his wife, to Samuel Withers - reference to a sale made 15 Mar. 1678/9 from Humphrey Davenport, Chyrurgion, to Robert Page of Kent County, Province of Md. - part of "Maiden Poynt" on south side St. Michael's River - Mary Beck being the sole heiress of Robert Page. Wit: John Wrightson, James Benson.

116 Last day of January 1686 John Standly and Judith his wife, and Christopher Bateson and Hannah his wife, to Henry Boston, Carpenter - 300 acres called "Timber Neck" on a branch of St. Michael's Creek - laid out for Standly and Bateson. Wit: William Bird, Thomas Delehay. Acknowledged before Edward Man and George Robins.

117 9 Oct. 1686 John Reynolds of Kent County, Territory of Pennsylvania, Planter, to James Hall of Talbot, Planter - P/A to demand of James Benson, Chyrurgion, 7000 lbs. of tobacco and to make over a deed of sale. Wit: Samuel Payen, John Greer, Christopher May. Proven before George Robotham and George Robins.

118 26 July 1686 John Reynolds of Talbot, now of St. Jones, Territory of Pennsylvania, Planter, to James Benson, Chyrurgion - 50 acres on the south side of St. Michael's River called "Fox Harbour" - also 50 acres, a moiety of 100 acres called "Bogg Hole" - adjoining "Fox Harbour" and now in the tenure of James Benson. Wit: Sarah Hall, James Hall.

119 6 Nov. 1687 John Harwood, son and heir of Robert Harwood of Talbot, deceased, to Clement Sale, Planter - referes to the sale of 300 acres called "Cottingham," made 12 Nov. 1668 by Isack Abraham to Robert Harwood - the said land on a branch of St. Michael's River adjoining the land of John Cinamount. Also 100 acres called "Harwood's Hill" about

a mile from St. Michael's River - patented to Robert Harwood. Wit: R. Gouldsbrough, Jacob Abraham, Thomas Brouff.

15 Nov. 1687 Peter Sayer, Sheriff, to Clement Sale - receipt for 12 shillings - alienation money.

121 (no date) Hester Grosse to Richard Wynne - P/A to sell in her name 300 acres called "Gross Coate" and 24 acres called "Gross' Addition." Wit: Edward Overing, Francis Lather.

122 17 Oct. 1687 Henrietta Maria Lloyd from William Grosse and Hester his wife - 300 acres called "Gross Coate" on the north side of Morgan's Creek in St. Michael's River - also "Gross' Addition" om Lloyd's Creek in Wye River, containing 24 acres as by certificate dated 22 April 1684.

123 9 Oct. 1687 Hester Gross to Richard Bennett - P/A to convey 200 acres called "Abbinton" in the northern branch of Wye River, in the woods. Wit: Edward Overing, Francis Lather.

124 12 Nov. 1687 Richard Wynne of Talbot County from William Gross and Hester his wife - moiety of "Abbinton" on northern branch of Wye River in the woods - on the east side of land laid out for John Write and adjoining the lands of William Jones and Peter Sides - being 200 acres, part of 400 acres. Wit: David Mackelfresh, Susannah Lowe.

125 __ Nov. 1687 Edmund O'Dwyer, Innholder, to Peter Sayer, Gent. - 50 acres at the mouth of Wye River called "Crouch'es Island" - mentioned in a patent for "Crouch'es Choice" formerly belonging to Josias Crouch. Wit: Ignatius Craycroft, William Hemsley, Flo. Sullivane.

126 16 Oct. 1687 Thomas Briges, Planter, to Stephen Bridge - in exchange for certain land sold to him by Stephen Bridge, being the third share of 500 acres - deeds 100 acres in Talbot County on Bridges' Cove and Bridges' Point and Phillips' Cove. Wit: Thos. Collins, Wm. Clark.

128 14 Nov. 1687 Charles Hollingsworth, Planter, to Robert Smith, Gent. - 300 acres of land on Chester River - according to patent. Wit: William Hackett, Nathaniel Wright.

129 16 Aug. 1687 Samuel Taylor, Planter, to Vincent Lowe - 500 acres on the south side of Parrott's Branch adjoining William Parrott, east side of Tradehaven Creek. Also 80 acres called "The Addition" - east side of Tredhaven Creek adjoining land formerly laid out for Samuel Taylor and adjoining the lands of Thomas Taylor. Vincent Lowe conveys to Samuel Taylor, 1000 acres called "Arcady" on Elliott's Branch in Chester River. Wit: Nico. Lowe, R. Gouldesborough, Robert Smith.

130 14 Nov. 1687 Robert Smith to Charles Hollingsworth, Planter - 239 acres on a branch of Island Creek in Chester River called "Smith's Forrest." Wit: William Hackett, Nathaniel Wright.

13 Nov. 1687 Anna Smith to Thomas Collins - P/A. Wit: Edward Slado, Thomas Bruff.

130   15 Nov. 1687   Elizabeth Lowe to her brother-in-law Michael Turbutt -
P/A to convey "Piney Neck" to John Miells. Wit: James Murphy, Charles
Robinson.

131   15 Nov. 1687   Hon. Vincent Lowe, Esq., to John Miles of Talbot - 200
acres between Cheasopeacke Bay and Harris' Mannor called "Pinney Neck" -
Wit: James Murphey, Charles Robinson.

132   21 June 1687   William Cowell to Nathaniel Wright - 300 acres, "Tully's
Reserve," on the south side of the eastern branch of Coursica Creek -
formerly laid out for Stephen Tully. Wit: George Barlow, Ann Wright,
Mary Willson.

134   17 Oct. 1687   Stephen Bridges of Talbot, Planter, to Thomas Bridges -
in consideration of land sold to him by Thomas Bridges - conveys part
of "Ditteridge" at the head of the northeast branch of Wye River. Wit:
Thomas Collins, William Clarke.

135   15 Nov. 1687   Josias Crouch of Talbot to Edmund Dwyer - 150 acres called
"Crouche's Choyce" at the mouth of Wye River - adjoining the land laid
out for Henry Morgan. Also "Crouch'es Island" in the mouth of the Wye
River. Wit: Richard Hazledine, Flo. Sullivane, Timothy Donovan.

136   13 Nov. 1687   Robert Smith, Gent., to John Davis - 200 acres called
"Smith's Poligon" adjoining land laid out for William Smith, Bruff's
land and Deney's land. Wit: Edward Slade, Thomas Bruff. Anna Smith to
Thomas Collins - P/A.

137   13 Nov. 1687   Anna Smith to Thomas Collins - P/A to convey in her name
200 acres of land to Philip Hopkins. Wit: Edward Slade, Thos. Bruff.

137   15 Nov. 1687   Edmund O'Dwyer to Josias Crouch - bond of assurance -
Crouch having sold to O'Dwyer 150 acres of land and 50 acres was taken
and surveyed for the town of Doncaster in Wye River - of which Josias
Crouch has sold 1 lot to Madam Henrietta Maria Lloyd; 1 lot to William
Dixon; 1 lot to John Davis; 1 to Henry Costin; 1 to James Clayland; as
also to the orphan of Bryan Omealy - O'Dwyer releases any claim to the
lots sold and to let Josias Crouch have a bureing (sic) place of four-
teen yards square where the former wife of Crouch is buried. Wit: Flo.
Sullivane, Thomas Bruff, Richard Hazledine.

138   15 Nov. 1687   Josias Crouch and Mary his wife, to Edmund Dwyer - 100
acres called "Liberty" - adjoining the lands of John Glandening and
Coll. Coursey. Wit: Richard Hazledine, Flo. Sullivane, Timothy Duna-
van.

139   14 Nov. 1687   Michael Powell Vanderfort to Robert Smith, Gent. - 350
acres on a branch of Wye River called "Vanderfort." Wit: John Jackson,
Thomas Bridges.

140   20 Sept. 1687   George Bowes, Planter, and Margaret his wife, to David
Rogers - 280 acres called "Moorefields" - in the woods on the west side

of Tuckahoe Creek - at the head of "Smith's Clifts" on the east - adjoining "Dunmore Heath" and the land called "Framptom." Wit: John Baynard, Thomas Allcocke, Nathaniel Wright.

141 16 Aug. 1687 Richard Dudley, Tailer, to John Dun - bond. Wit: John Baynard, Thomas Allcocke, Nathaniel Wright.

Richard Dudley and Ellinor his wife, to John Dunn - 200 acres, "Dudley's Clifts" on a branch of Tuckahoe Creek - adjoining "Smith's Clifts" and Land of Peter Sharpe called "Chestnut Bay." Same witnesses as above.

142 16 Mar. 1686 William Snelling, Boatwright, and Margaret his wife, to Robert Grundy of Talbot, Merchant - 50 acres called "Endeavour" - on the north side of Choptank River - west side Tredhaven Creek adjoining the land laid out for Samuel Winslow called "Plain Dealing." Wit: Nico. Gouldsborough, Judith Gouldsborough.

143 17 June 1687 Robert Smith, Gent., to Samuel Wright, Planter - 100 acres in the woods - part of "Smith's Farm" and "Wrexam Plaines." Wit: John Hacker, David Blaney, Flo. Sullivane.

143 15 July 1686 John Acton of Annarundell County, Planter, and Margaret his wife, to William Troth, Planter - 300 acres of land called "Acton," patented to Richard Acton of Annarundell Co., deceased, father of the said John, 15 April 1671 - on the north side Choptank River adjoining land laid out for Alexander Jordan. Wit: Edward Dorsey, John Swallow.

144 8 Feb. 1686 John Acton acknowledged before Edward Mann and George Robins, two of his Majestie's Justices.

144 20 Dec. 1689 John Harwood, Planter, to John Dams, Planter - 100 acres called "Rich Farm" on the fresh runs of King's Creek - adjoining land laid out for Robert Harwood. Wit: William Finney, J. Delehay.

145 26 July 1686 John Reynolds, late of Talbot, Now of St. Jones in the Territory of Pennsylvania, Planter - to James Benson of Talbot, Chyrurgion - 50 acres called "Fox Harbour." ("This is a mistake, entered before." sic)

145. 21 Dec. 1684 James Peacock of Stockton Upon Tease, Co. Durham, Master and Mariner, to Thomas Cook, same town and county, Shipwright and Hester his wife - 400 acres on the east side of the northeast branch of King's Creek - reference to patent granted 1 Aug. 1673 to Henry Parker for a tract called "Parker's Lott." Wit: Richard Watts, John Rudel.

147 22 Mar. 1687 George Aldridge, Carpenter, to Richard Sweatman - one-half of land laid out for George Aldridge late of Talbot, since then deceased, father of the said grantor George Aldridge, 350 acres called "Indian Neck" near Back Wye River - adjoining land laid out for Jonathon Hopkinson since deceased and land of Atwell Bodell, called "Bodell" - bounded on the east by land of Richard Walemer(?) - on the north by "Hopton" - on the west by Back Wye. Wit: Griffith Jones, Samuel Withers, Kym Mabbott.

149 16 Feb. 1688 Joseph Sampele of St. Mary's County, Chyrurgion and Mary
his wife, to James Ross of Talbot, Chyrurgion - consideration twenty
five pounds lawful money of England - part of a tract at the head of the
fresh runs of Wye River - formerly taken up by William Finney - called
"Finney's Hermitage" and containing 200 acres - formerly in the occupation of William Watkins and given to the said Joseph Sampele by William
Finney in frank marriage of his daughter now wife of Joseph Sampele by
a deed dated 26 Feb. 1683. Wit: Wm. Harris, Charles Furrol. Sig: JO-
SEPH SAMPLE.

150 29 Oct. 1684 Richard Carter of London, Merchant, to Timothy Dunnamon,
Province of Maryland, Cooper - part of "Carter's Rich Farme" at the head
of St. Michael's River adjoining Benjamin Pride's Branch and the Upper
Plantation Branch - containing 200 acres. Wit: Wm. Helmsley, Jr., John
Morgin, Francis Storey. Anthony Rumball, Factor, given P/A, 21 July last
past.

150 27 Oct. 1687 Robert Smith and Anna his wife, to Philip Hopkins - "Brom-
ley" in Wye River, on Williams' Branch - granted to Henry Parker by a
patent issued 10 Aug. 1683 for 200 acres - adjoining Thomas Williams,
Wm. Coursey and Henry Costin. Wit: Arent Grandures, Sarah Bankes.

151 14 Oct. 1687 Thomas Russum, Planter, and Elizabeth his wife, one of the
daughters and co-heir of John Morris late of Thirdhaven, Planter, de-
ceased, to Peter Anderton of Thirdhaven, Carpenter - 300 acres called
"Foxhole" in the mouth of the Thirdhaven Creek and adjoining to Foxhole
Branch. Also a moiety of "Fox Harbour," 100 acres in the mouth of
Thirdhaven Creek - adjoining the land laid out for Richard White and
Thomas Phillips. Wit: Sam Withers, Phillip Salter.

152 4 Oct. 1687 Thomas Hutchinson and Dorothy his wife, to Samuel Abbot -
Sr., Planter - 100 acres in Island Creek, Choptank River, part of
"Hull's Addition" and also part of "Barnston" - adjoining Samuel Abbot's
land, "Abbington" and "Buckroe" - containing 100 acres. Wit: Anthony
Cox, Samuel Abbott, Jr., Thomas Robins. Acknowledge before Edward Mann
and George Robins.

153 25 Jan. 1687 Thomas Hutchinson to Robert Jones, Blacksmith.- part of
"Hull" and part of "Hull's Addition" - adjoining "Boon's Hope" now in
tenure of Clement Sale and the land of Samuel Abbot called "Buckroe,"
Same witnesses as above.

154 10 Jan. 1687 Thomas Hutchinson and Dorothy his wife, to Samuel Abbot,
Jr. - 150 acres called "Hutchinson's Addition" - north side Choptank
River on a branch of St. Michael's Creek - adjoining "Lord's Gift"
laid out for Thomas Hutchinson, and the land of William Rich. Wit:
Robert Jones, Samuel Abbot, Sr., Thomas Robins.

155 10 Jan. 1687 Thomas Hutchinson and Dorothy his wife, to Anthony Cox -
100 acres, "Barnston" on Island Creek, Great Choptank River - adjoining
Samuel Abbot. Wit: Robt. Jones, Sam'l. Abbot, Sr., Thomas Robins.

156 10 Feb. 1687 Thomas Hutchinson and Dorothy his wife, to John Cliffe,

Planter - 100 acres at the head of Island Creek called "Hutchinson's Plaines" and part of "Barnestone" - adjoining the land of Anthony Cox, and Samuel Abbot's "Abbington." Wit: R. Jones, A. Cox, T. Robins.

10 Feb. 1687 Thomas Hutchinson and Dorothy his wife, to Thomas Browne - 100 acres on a branch of St. Michael's Creek called "Lord's Gift." Wit: R. Jones, A. Cox, T. Robins.

157 8 Mar. 1687 William Sharp to Henry Alexander - reference to a grant made by Cecilius, Lord Baron of Baltimore, to James Furbus late of this Province, for 100 acres called "Whales" - at the head of Dividing Creek - the present Lord Baltimore has by a writ of Mandamus to inquire into the state of the land to two Justices who reported that James Furbus was dead; the land was escheated and granted to William Sharp, Merchant. Wit: John Games, David Hould. Acknowledged before Edward Man and William Combes.

159 12 Nov. 1687 John Davis of Dorchester Co., Planter, to Richard White of Bullinbrooke Creek, Planter - parcel of land divided from the land of Edward Rooper by a line of trees - lying on the north side - formerly sold by Richard White to John Davis. Wit: Edward Lydenham, Richard Hewes.

159 17 Jan. 1687 John Pitt, Planter, and Sarah his wife, to Edward Turner, Planter - 400 acres called "John's Hill" in a branch of King's Creek, Great Choptank River - adjoining Henry Parker's land called "Parker's Freshes." Surveyed 10 Aug. 1675. Wit: George Goulte, Sam'l. Brodewee.

160 19 Mar. 1687 Robert Smyth of Talbot, Gent., and Anna his wife, to Henry Price, Planter - 200 acres called "Smith's Farm" on the eastern branch of Corsica Creek - at the head of the White Marsh - adjoining the lands of Samuel Wright and land laid out for William Hemsley. Wit: M. Miller, John Johnson.

19 Mar. 1687 Robert Smyth and Anna his wife, to Richard Myrex, Planter - 300 acres in a branch of Corsica Creek, part of "Wrexam Plaines" and "Smith's Forrest." Wit: M. Miller, J. Johnson.

161 2 Feb. 1687 Vincent Lowe, Esq., and Elizabeth his wife, to John Lane, Planter - 200 acres called "Long Benington" on the north side of Tuckahoe Creek adjoining land laid out for _____ Toleson. Wit: Nicholas Lowe, Robert Gouldesborough.

162 29 Mar. 1687 Peter Sayer, Gent., to Thomas Hind of Drougheda, Kingdom of Ireland, Merchant - "Beedles' Outlet," 400 acres on a marked road from Wye River to Chester River - adjoining the land of Henry Coursey, Esq. Wit: Thomas Smithson, Thomas Bruff, Flo. Sullivane.

163 4 Nov. 1687 James Wasse to Coll. Vincent Lowe of Talbot County, Prov. of Maryland - P/A - granted before Nicholas Hayward, Notary Public in London, England - declaring he had not heard from Daniel Toas, William Johnson, William Perry and John Pitt to whom he had committed his inquiry - to accompt for his affairs relating to his plantation in Maryland and particularly of Daniel Carnell, administrator of Richard Mich-

el late of Tredhaven Creek in Choptank River, deceased - to inquire what estate Mitchell had purchased or took up during his lifetime either in Maryland or Pennsilvania and what estate Richard Michel and Mary his wife had at the time of his decease, either real or personally - also to inquire and demand of the heirs, executors or administrators of the said Richard Michell and of the said Mary Michell a true and just account of what they dyed worth, either in Md., Penna. or elsewhere - in regard to articles dated 15th Xber (Dec.) 1679 made between Wasse and Michell - among other things agreed that Richard Mitchell at his own expense transport himself, his wife and child into Maryland and there settle on and manage the plantation of James Wasse called "Ratcliffe Mannor" in Tredhaven Creek and that Wasse should receive one full moiety or half part of all the gain and profit which Michell, his family or servants should make upon the said plantation by any manner of labor, misery or industry whatsoever and that the servants, household stuff, stock, chattels, goods, debts and effects on the plantation with all of the estate of the said Richard Michell in the hands of any person proceding from the pains, care, industry and endeavour should be equally parted, shared and divided between James Wasse and Richard Michell - Michell covenanting to pay several debts due in Maryland on account of the plantation and from time to time purchase servants for the supply and management thereof - to continue and preserve the stock and to furnish and maintain the family and servants with apparell, food and other necessities and to pay the yearly quitrent to Lord Baltimore and to repair and amend all the houses, buildings and fences at his own cost and to inhabit upon the plantation with his family and servants during the term of eleven years if he should live so long and not to leave but to use his best skill for the management, and improvement of the plantation. Michell further promises to pay one equal moiety of all gains and profits and to render a yearly account of all transactions and of the condition of the plantation and also what gains or improvements he has made or hopes to make - Coll. Lowe to inquire how far Richard Michell and Mary his wife have followed the said articles and to demand an account from their heirs or administrators. In case of refusal Lowe to put into suit a bond of five hundred pounds - (₤500) given by Richard Mitchell for his true performance of the articles and to make an inventory of all chattels, cattle, goods and other things belonging to the plantation. Lowe to sell and dispose of the said plantation, houseing, stock and premises to any person for two hundred pounds (₤200) sterling and not under, or else suffer tenants to dwell on the several plantations and pay rent. Wit: Mark Alderig, Richard Roustone, Will. Alderne, Rebecca Alderne.

165 3 Mar. 1688 Thomas Clemens to Ambrose Ford - a parcel called _____ on Treadhaven Creek - adjoining the land of Anthony Griffith - containing 100 acres - mentions Parrott's Branch. Wit: Joseph Wiggot, Thomas Benit, Lambert Clemens.

165 19 June 1687 Francis Shepheard of Chester River, Planter and wife, to Richard Swan, Tailor - 200 acres on south side Chester River, called "Hemsley's Folly." Wit: John Wittinhall, Henry Cosden.

166 12 May 1688 John Davis of Virginia to Christopher Denny - "The White Clifts" according to patent - on Chester River adjoining the land of

Richard Tilghman. Wit: John Neall, James Greenwood.

167 22 June 1688 Hugh Paxton to John Clemens and Theophilus Davis - tract
on a branch of Wye River near the road - reference to patent. Wit:
Robert Smith, Nic. Lowe.

168 19 June 1688 Peter Dod and Elizabeth his wife, to Christopher Spry,
Planter - "Bodinton" - on a branch of Chester River called Brewer's
Branch - reference to patent. Wit: Thos. Smithson, Jno. Chaires.

168 16 June 1688 Richard Dudley, Tailor, and Ellinor his wife, to John
Ivritt, Parish of Stephen Heath, Middlesex County (Eng.), Mariner -
200 acres, "Dudley's Demaines" - in the woods at the head of a branch
of Tuckahoe Creek - adjoining "Dudley's Choice" and land called "Bugby." Wit: John Needles, John Pemberton.

169 22 June 1688 Thomas Bruff to John Lydel - "Cover Point" in Coursegall
Creek - the first bounder on Fishing Cove. reference to patent. Wit:
William Coursey, Nathaniel Wright, Robert Burman.

170 19 June 1688 Christopher Denny of Chester River, Planter, to Michael
Earle - "Woodland Neck," 100 acres - "Smith's Lott," 200 acres - on
the west side of Coursegall Creek. Anna, wife of Christopher Denny.
Wit: Thomas Bruff, Flo. Sullivane.

171 18 May 1688 John Richards, Carpenter, to George Goult, Planter - 200
acres, the moyety of 400 acres called ."Milford" on the east side of
Tuckahoe Creek. Anna, wife of John Richards. Wit: R. Gouldesborough,
Robert Smith.

172 20 June 1688 Robert Smith and Anne his wife, to John Davis of Talbot,
Planter - 200 acres called "Smith's Farm" on the eastern branch of
Coursica Creek Wit: John Lamb, Will. Hollinsworth.

172 20 Mar. 1687 Griffith Jones, Gent., Attorney for Stephen Tully, to
John Pooly, Planter - "Tully's Addition" and "Sandwich" the metes and
bounds according to patent. Wit: Thomas Bruff, Florence Sullivane.

173 29 May 1688 John Numan of St. Michael's River, Planter, and Mary his
wife, to Richard Carter, Merchant - Carter to lease to Numan part of
the land, one 40-foot tobacco house and to clear enough ground adjoining to it for 20,000 tobacco plants for one crop of tobacco or English
grain to be planted thereon; or seven houses, completed and finished
the next year ensuing. Also Nunam's dwelling plantation and the land
adjoining called "Good Chance" - 50 acres on the north side of the
eastern branch of St. Michael's River adjoining to the south the land
of Jacob Abrahams called "Cottingham" - on the east by the land of
Henrietta Maria Lloyd called "Partnership" - also 50 acres adjoining
Abrahams and "Good Chance" - called "Newnam's Thickett." Wit: Thomas
Smithson, Thomas Bessike, William Allen.

175 ___ June 1684 John Lillingston to John Ingram - 150 acres called "Bridge
North" - on Mill Branch of Coursegall Creek - adjoining "Ninevah."
Wit: Thomas Vaughn, Robert Mackline, John Robins.

176 9 Jan. 1688 Priscilla Thomson, widow, to Robert Smith - land sold by
Mrs. Mary Tilghman, widow, to Zachara Thomson and by his will devised
to Priscilla - 250 acres on Royston's Creek in Chester River. Wit:
Thomas Hines, Walter Smith.

176 10 June 1688 Francis Shepheard to Thomas Colney - 200 acres called
"Shepherd's Forest" in Double Creek, Chester River. Wit: James Smith,
John Wettinhall.

177 10 Apr. 1687 Daniel Walker, executor of Henry Parker, Gent., deceased,
to Richard Austin, Planter - 200 acres called "Fishing Bay" - sold by
Parker to Richard Austin, 6 Oct. 1686 - excepting that neck in the possession of Michael Russel containing 12 acres. Wit: Henry Adcock,
Richard Dearden.

178 22 Aug. 1688 George Parrott, Planter, and Elizabeth his wife, to John
Eason, Planter - "Poplar Levell" - 116 acres in the woods on a branch
of the Beaver Dam of King's Creek - on the northernmost branch near the
Tuckahoe road and a road called Old Mill Road. Wit: John Morrogh, Jacob Abrahams.

179 14 Aug. 1688 John Davis to John Morgan, Planter - 106 acres called
"Dunfield" near the head of Wye River in Talbot - adjoining Mrs. Brewer's and Henry Parker's land. Wit: Christopher Higgs, Ann Lodman.

180 21 Aug. 1688 John Wotters, Planter, and Martha his wife, to Henry Aylor, Planter - a moiety or one-half of "Buckby als Buckly"- on the west
side of Tuckahoe Creek back of "Smith's Clifts." Mentions a division
between Aylor and Roland Hambridge, containing 200 acres. Wit: Daniel
Morry, Jonathon Arey, John Richards.

180 20 Aug. 1688 William Kemp and Rebecca his wife of Kent Island, to
Robert Smith - 100 acres according to patent on Coursegal Creek formerly surveyed for Edward Burton, father of the said Rebecca Kemp - adjoining "Guiter's Harbour" on Coursegal Creek. Wit: Nic. Clouds, Solomon Wright.

181 20 July 1688 James Frisbey of Cecil County and Sarah his wife, to my
friend and brother-in-law Jacob Abrahams - P/A to acknowledge a parcel
of land sold to John Boram. Wit: William Sharp, Brion O'Brine. Proved
in open court - Nicholas Lowe, Clk.

181 20 July 1688 James Frisbey of Cecil County, and Sarah, his wife, to
John Boram - a moiety described in a deed of gift given by George Read
to his two brothers, William and Thomas Read - the moiety by the will
of Thomas Read was given to his sister Sarah, now wife of James Frisbey -
being part of "Ridley" - 300 acres. Wit: William Sharp, Brion O'Brion,
William Nouell.

182 Thomas Faulkner, Carpenter, to John Burnam, Planter - bond. Wit:
Thomas Beswicke, Francis Story. 19 July 1688.

182 19 July 1688 Thomas Faulkner, Carpenter, and Anne his wife, to John

Burnam - 200 acres of rough, uncultivated land on a branch of St. Michael's River, called "Faulkner's Square" - adjoining "Carter's Farm."
Wit: Thomas Besswicke, John Daley.

183 21 Aug. 1688 John Wotters and Martha his wife, to Roland Hambridge, Millwright - 200 acres - a moiety of 400 acres called "Buckby" or "Buckley" near "Smith's Clifts" on Tuckahoe Creek - adjoining the land of Henry Ayler. Wit: Jonathon Arey, Daniel Morry, John Richards.

185 18 Aug. 1688 William Hackett of Chester River to William Hill - 150 acres called "Barton" - south side Chester River on a branch of Hambleton's Creek adjoining the land of Richard Collins called "Collins his Lott." Wit: Thomas Ford, Solomon Wright.

187 19 Aug. 1688 John Newnam of St. Michael's River, Planter, and Mary his wife, to John Stacey and Thomas Gully, Planters. 100 acres called "Bobbshill" in Woodenhawk Branch of King's Creek. Wit: Anthony Rumball, William Allen.

186 25 Aug. 1688 Thomas Bruff and Rhoda his wife, to James Meend - 150 acres called "Highfield" at the head of a small run of Tuckahoe Creek. Wit: James Downes, John Thrift, Christopher Denny.

190 19 Aug. 1688 Jacob Abrahams of St. Michael's River, Planter, and Elizabeth his wife, to Thomas Ubankes of Talbot - a moiety of 400 acres in the forest called "Jacob and John's Pasture" - near the head of St. Michael's River between Richard Carter's land called "Carter's Plains," "Omaly's Range" and the Court Road - laid out to Jacob Abrahams and John Newnam. Wit: John Morrough, John Eason.

191 21 Aug. 1688 Robert Devenish of Talbot and Ann his wife, to John Roads, Cooper - 150 acres called "Wattson" on the west side of Cuthbert's Cove an adjoining the land of Cuthbert Phelps. Wit: Nic. Lowe, Thomas Tate.

192 20 Aug. 1688 Robert Smith and Ann his wife, to Henry Green, Planter - 100 acres, part of "Wrexam Plaines" - adjoining the land of Richard Mirax and another plantation adjoining land laid out for Stephen Tully, containing 200 acres. Wit: Philip Healeadgia, Nicholas Cloud.

193 14 Aug. 1688 Isaak Stone to Robert Norrest - 200 acres on a branch of Coursica Creek adjoining "Tully's Reserve" laid out for Stephen Tully, purchased of Robert Smith. Wit: Solomon Wright, William Hackett.

196 17 Aug. 1688 Catherine Hackett wife of William, to Thomas Collins - P/A to acknowledge a sale made by her husband to Thomas Ford. Wit: Thomas Besswick.

196 17 Aug. 1688 William Hackett and Cathrine his wife, to Thomas Ford - 155 acres called "Southamton" - in Chester River, north side of Hambleton's Branch adjoining Barton's land. Wit: Solomon Wright, Robt. Norrest.

197   27 Apr. 1688 Thomas Hutchinson, Tanner, and Dorothy his wife, to Joshua
      Attkins - 70 acres called "Hull" in a branch of Island Creek called
      Croock's Branch and adjoining a parcel bought of Hutchinson by Robert
      Jones, Blacksmith. Wit: John Swallow, Richard France. Dorothy acknow-
      ledged the deed before Edw. Man and George Robins, Justices.

199   7 Sept. 1688 Robert Smith, Gent., to Samuel Wright, Planter - 200 acres
      adjoining "Smith's Forrest." Wit: John Madbery, Richard Austyn, Flo.
      Sullivane.

200   18 Sept. 1688 John Gatterly of Chester River to Thomas Bruff - 200
      acres called "Chestnut Meadow" - west side of the northernmost branch
      of Tuckahoe Creek - adjoining "Providence," formerly laid out for Steph-
      en Tully - "Chestnut Meadow" formerly laid out for John Robinson and
      sold to John Gatterly. Wit: Michael Earle, James Ross, Will. Dixon.

201   18 Sept. 1688 Henry Aylor, Planter, to George Bowes - 100 acres, "Sib-
      land" adjoining Bowes' land called "Maxfield" and a part of "Sibland"
      already in his possession - west side Tuckahoe Creek. Wit: John Standley,
      Francis Vickars.

202   4th day 4th mo 1688 Thomas Vaughn's deposition re' a parcel of land laid
      out for Thomas Vaughn and Richard Gurling on the Choptank River between
      "Dover" and "Boston Clift."

202   18 Sept. 1688 Judith Hemsley to Ann Dayly, wife of John Dayly, Planter -
      gift of 2 cows, a young sow with pigg. T. Delehay, Jas. Clayland.

203   12 Nov. 1688 William Jones, Planter, and Jone his wife, to William
      Troth, Gent. - 100 acres according to patent - "Mt. Hope." Wit: Nico.
      Lowe, John Lundigan, John Robins.

204   20 Jan. 1688 Robert Devenish, Planter, and Ann his wife, to Jeremiah
      Thomas - 500 acres, "Devenish's Chance" on the Unicorne Branch, Chester
      River - adjoining the land of Francis Shepard called "Shepard's Field."
      Wit: Thos. Bridges, Thomas Bridal. Bond witnessed by Robert Towe and
      James Costerley.

205   13 Nov. 1688 John Richards of Talbot, Planter, and Ann his wife, to
      George Pratt - 200 acres called "Millford" on the east side of Tuckahoe
      Creek at the mouth of Morgan's Creek. Wit: Christopher Denny, John
      Duckworth, John Baynard.

206   20 Nov. 1688 Benjamin Parratt, Planter, and Elizabeth his wife, to
      Robert Frampton, Planter - "Collins' Pasture" at the head of a branch of
      Highfield Creek issuing out of Tuckahoe Creek - adjoining "Parrott's
      Reserve" - containing 50 acres. Wit: Christopher Denny, John Duckworth,
      John Baynard.

207   20 Nov. 1688 Robert Devenish and Ann his wife, to Thomas Barratt of
      Kent County, Planter - 200 acres, "Lambeth," on the east side of the
      Unicorn Branch, Chester River. Wit: John Eason, Thomas Bridges. Bond
      witnessed by Robert Towe and James Costley.

208 20 Nov. 1686 Francis Collins, Planter, to Benjamin Parratt - "Collins'
Pasture" - in the woods near a branch of Tuckahoe. Wit: Samuel Broadway, William Barnes.

209 4 Oct. 1688 Thomas Hutchinson of West Jersey, late of Talbot County,
Tanner, and Dorothy his wife, to Nicholas Lowe - the plantation whereon
I lately dwelt - a tract of land formerly laid out for Miles Cook, Marriner - 1000 acres called "Cook's Hope" and by Dorothy, relict of Miles
Cook, sold to John Edmondson, Merchant and by Edmondson to Hutchinson -
on Treadhaven Creek - mentions the dwelling plantation of Emanuel Jenkinson and Roger Summers but now called "James Edmondson's Lower Plantation" and "John Edmondson's Negro Quarters"- mentions a branch of the
creek near which John Stanley now dwelleth - containing and now laid out
for 200 acres. Thomas Hutchinson's signature witnessed by Judith Gouldesborough, John Man and Thomas Hale. Dorothy Hutchinson's signature witnessed by William Lasmell and Nicholas North.

210 16 Jan. 1688 John Emerson of Talbot, Planter, son of Thomas Emerson of
Annarundell County, deceased, to William Hemsley, Jr. - moiety of a
tract of land laid out for Thomas Carew of London, Merchant - in Wye River on Coll. Lloyd's Island - devised to Thomas and John Emerson - 1000
acres to be divided. Thomas Emerson sold to William Hemsley. Wit:
Isaac Winchester, Samuel Payne.

15 Jan. 1688 Elizabeth Silvester, wife of James Silvester, to John Baynard - P/A. Wit: George Dohorty, Thomas Hemsley.

211 15 Jan. 1688 James Silvester, Carpenter, and Elizabeth his wife, to
Timothy Lane, Planter - 110 acres, "Silvester's Forrest" in the fork
between Choptank River and Tokahoe Creek - adjoining "Gravely How."
Also "Sylvester's Addition," 300 acres - mentions a bounded tree of Eman-
uel Jenkinson's land. Witness for James Sylvester: John Laine and
Dorothy Gren_ar. Witness for Elizabeth: R. Gouldesborough, John N____r,
Dennis Connolly.

212 13 Nov. 1688 William Scott, Carpenter, son of John Scott and Margaret
his wife, deceased, to William Hemsley - "Hambleton's Park" at the head
of Wye River. Wit: Andrew Price, John Dine

212 1 Jan. 1688 Richard Dudley, Tailor, and Elinor his wife, to Jonathon
Arey and David Arey, Planters - 100 acres called "Dudley's Choice" on
the west side Tokahoe Creek on the back of the land laid out for John
Pawson - mentions Haman's Branch. Wit: John Baynard, James Sillvester,
Moses Sherry.

___ Jan. 1688 Margaret Smith, wife of James Smith, to Robert Smith -P/A
to convey "Smith Field" on the Red Lyon Branch, Chester River.

213 7 Jan. 1688 James Smith and Margrett his wife, to Will Aston - 200 acres
called "Smith Field" in Chester River, Red Lyon Branch. Wit: Richard
Skinner, John Pearle.

214 16 Jan. 1688 William Hemsley, Planter, to John Emerson - part of "Ham-

bleton's Park" and part of "Hemsley's Addition" in Wye River on Bread and Cheese Harbour Branch - mentions "Piney Point" and the plantation of John Dames - containing 150 acres. Wit: Isaac Winchester, Samuel Payne.

214 __ Dec. 1688 George Hurlock, Planter, to Moses Dunkley of Kent Co., Province of Maryland - 200 acres called "Bloomsbury" on a branch of King's Creek - adjoining John Browne's land called "Browne's Lott." Wit: John Walker, Robert Towe, Will. Coxell, Petter Dod.

215 24 day 5 month 1688 William Southbe, County of Philadelphia in Pennsilvania, to John Pitt - P/A to convey 100 acres to Thomas Tylar. Wit: Samuel Richardson, John Shillson.

215 18 day 4 month called June 1688 William Southbe of John's Creek, Delaway Bay, Boatwright, to Thomas Tyler - land in King's Creek adjoining "Parker's Park" - the land of John Ashdell (200 acres out of a patent for 300 acres called "Kingston") - this tract being the other 100 acres of "Kingston." Wit: John Juell, John Browne.

216 15 Jan. 1688 William Darvall of Kent Co., Territory of Pennsilvania, Merchant, to John Lane - P/A to convey 50 acres to Robert Poor of Talbot, Planter. Wit: John Baynard, James Sillvester, George Dohority.

216 15 Jan. 1688 William Darvall of Kent, Territory of Pennsilvania, Merchant, to Robert Poor, Planter - 50 acres called "Waterford" which is part of "Hackfield" late in the tenure of William Hill - on the east side of Tokahoe Creek. Wit: John Baynard, James Sylvester, George Dohority. Rebeckah, wife of William Darvall, agrees to the sale.

217 17 day 10th month 1686 William Hill, Kent County, Territory of Pennsilvania to William Purnell and Richard Purnell - P/A.

15 Nov. 1685 William Hill, Sr., Kent County, Territory of Pennsilvania, Planter, to James Sylvester - 100 acres called "Hill's Outlet" on the north side of Choptank River, east side of Tockahoe Creek - at the head of the land laid out for Nicholas Hackett, now in possession of Wm. Hill - near Morgan's Creek. Wit: Thomas Thurston, Walter Thomas.

218 __ Mar. 1688 Richard Swann, Sadler, and Ann his wife, to Thomas Bruff, Innholder - 200 acres on the south side Chester River called "Ramsey's Folly." Wit: James Ross, Den. Connolly.

218 6 Feb. 1688 John Bird of Talbot, lately of Annarundell Co., Gent., and Elizabeth his wife, to John Howell of Stockton, Kingdom of England - in consideration of ₤40 lawful money of England - "Turner's Ridge" at the head of Wye River in the woods and adjoining land laid out for Thomas Francis, 200 acres - also "Planter's Increase" in the woods, adjoining land laid out for William Jones and Petter Sides called "Planter's Delight" - 100 acres. Wit: Daniel Toas, John Richardson, Griffith Jones. John Bird also sells livestock to Howell - schedule annexed.

219 20 Mar. 1688 Hon. Vincent Lowe, Esq., to Richard Bishopp, brother and heir to William Bishopp, late of Talbot, Gent., deceased - land in Talbot County on ye head of Chester River on the northwest branch - 500 acres called "Chesterfield." Wit: Nico. Lowe, Griff. Jones.

220 16 Mar. 1688 Ann Clemens, Spinster, to Thomas Clemens, Planter - 2/3 of "Worgan's Reserve" in King's Creek at the head of the northern branch containing 300 acres. Wit: Thomas Anderson, John Price, Richard Hews.

221 11 Dec. 1688 George Robins, Gent., and Margrett his wife, to John Waymouth, Planter - in consideration of 4000 lbs of tobacco; a cow with calf and a heifer with calf - sells 50 acres of "Hopkins Point" on the west side of Treadhaven Creek. Wit: Lambert Wilmer, Nicholas Gouldesborough, Judith Gouldesborough, George Robins, Jr.

221 1 Mar. 1688 George Pallmer of Talbot to Thomas Collins - 200 acres, part of "Spread Eagle" - adjoining Thomas Seward. Wit: John Lundy, Lar. Knowles.

222 19 Mar. 1688 Thomas Clements, Planter, to Thomas Cook, Planter and Shipwright and Hester his wife - 2/3 of "Worgan's Reserve," 300 acres in King's Creek. Wit: V. Hemsley, Thos. Anderson, John Price.

223 5 Mar. 1688 Francis Sheppard to James Davis, Planter - 100 acres between Unicorn Branch of the Chester River and ye land of Christopher Rousby - 400 acres, part of "Sheppard's Forrest." Wit: Thomas Collins, William Warren.

224 18 Mar. 1688 Mary Dwyer to Thomas Bruff - P/A - witnessed by Francis Kinaman, Christopher Pypard.

Edmund O'Dwyer, Gent., to Thomas Hinds of ye Kingdome of Ireland, Merchant - 100 acres called "Crouch's Choice" at the mouth of Wye River - adjoining the land formerly laid out for Henry Morgan. Wit: Christopher Pypard, Thomas Collins, Flo. Sullevane, Thomas Brierly.

225 28 Jan. 1688 Edmund O'Dwyer to Cathrine Sexton of the Bay Hundred - "Liberty," 100 acres in Talbot and adjoining the land in possession of John Glandening and Coll. Henry Coursey's land. Wit: Will. Coursey, Laur. Knowles.

225 20 May 1689 George Willson of Talbot, Planter, and Mary his wife, to Samuel Wright - 300 acres, "Walthrope" - formerly granted to Robert Page and by Matthew Ward, the assignee of George Jolly - adjoining John Winchester and land laid out for Henry Coursey - late in the occupation of George Willson and Mary his wife, daughter of Robert Page. Wit: Edward Noel, Flo. Sullevane, Barnard Griffin.

226 19 May 1689 William Hemsley, Planter, and Cornelia his wife, to John Thrift - 200 acres at the head of Wye River called "Hemsley's Arcadia"- adjoining "Normington," land in the possession of Warren Sudall and the land of Col. Lloyd called "Lloyd's Costin," Richard Peather and Rebecka Woollman. Wit: John Pooly, T. Delehay.

227 James Ferron, Carpenter, to Andrew Price, Gent. - P?A to convey to Michael Earle, Innholder - land called "Well's Neck" on Wye River - part of a parcel formerly belonging to Robert Smith, deceased - 128 acres bought of James Simons which by Letter of Attorney was acknowledged to me by John King - on Morgan's Creek. Wit: Walter Jones, Allis Jones.

16 May 1689 Andrew Price to Michael Earle - bond - Wit: William Elliott, Francis Bradley, Warner Sudall.

228 25 Apr. 1689 Thomas Hinds to Thomas Bruff - "Crouche's Choice" - purchased of Edmund O'Dwyer. Wit: Den(nis) Connolly, J. Downes, Frances Roe. On 27 Apr. 1689 Delivered by Hinds to Thomas Bruff. Wit: Christopher Pypard, James Clayland, Isaac Dixon, George Smith, Andrew Fallon.

229 10 May 1688 William Hatfield, Planter, and Elizabeth his wife, to John Thrift, Planter - 150 acres called "Normington" - at the head of Wye River on Bread and Cheese Harbour Branch. Wit: William Hemsley, T. Delehay.

230 20 May 1689 Samuell Wright to George Willson - 100 acres in Chester River - adjoining "Smith's Forrest." Wit: Edward Noell, Flo. Sullivane, Barnard Griffin.

231 29 May 1689 Petter Sayer, Gent., to Edmund O'Dwyer - 350 acres known as "Kirkham" - adjoining the land of Henry Morgan - patented to Martin Kirk and John Hill and assigned to Edmund Lackey and by him to Henry Taylor and lately in the occupation of Peter Sayer. Wit: John Hawkins, Thomas Harmon, Flo. Sullivane.

232 18 June 1689 Robert Boreman, Carpenter, to John Lane, Planter - "Kirkham's Lott" between the northeast branch of the Choptank River and Tokhoe - containing 200 acres; also "Goulden Lyon" containing 200 acres. Wit: Wm. Haress, John Smith.

233 Hannah Hamer, wife of John Hamer, to William Sparks - P/A. Wit: Richard Boreman, Denis Macarty.

1 May 1689 John Hamer and Hannah his wife, to William Bush - 200 acres called "Smith's Delight" in Chester River; also "Arcadia," on the northeast branch of Treadhaven Creek. Wit: Ambrose Kinemount, William Scott.

234 22 May 1689 John Lane, Planter, to William Ballford - 200 acres on east side Tokahoe Creek on Hill's Creek Branch - adjoining land laid out for Emanuel Jenkinson; land called "Edmondson's Green Close" the land of Henry Barker and John Morgan; and land laid out for Nicholas Hackett. Wit: Den. Connolly, Thomas Bruff.

235 18 June 1689 John Lane, Planter, and Mary his wife to Edward James of Kent Island - "Lane's Ridge" - in the woods between Choptank River and Tockahoe Creek - north side of St. Jones' Path. Adjoining

land laid out for William and Richard Purnell called "Purnell's Addition," containing 200 acres. Also "Castle Towne" - adjoining "Lane's Ridge" and "Purnell's Addition," 100 acres. Wit: Edward Pollard, Will. Coursey.

236 18 June 1689 John Lane, Planter, and Mary his wife, to William Jones of Talbot - 85 acres, part of "Lane's Forrest" in the fork between Choptank River and Tockahoe Creek. Wit: Edward Pollard, William Coursey.

237 24 day 5th month (July) 1689 William Southbe, County of Philadelphia, in Pennsylvania, to William Sharpe - P/A to convey part of "Readley" to John Dickinson - 150 acres. Wit: Da. Lloyd, Clk., Penna.

238 31 Aug. 1689 William Southbe, Jr. of Pennsylvania, Planter, to John Dickinson, Planter - 150 acres, the upper half of "Readley" - William Southbe, Jr. son of William, Sr. and Elizabeth, his mother, the only sister of George Read, William Read and Thomas Read. In 1674 George Read to William and Thomas, his brothers, 300 acres out of a patent for 800 laid out for Thomas Read of Calvert County, deceased, who was father of George (William and Thomas Read are deceased). Wit: William Sharpe, Jacob Abrahams.

239 8th month 1689 Abraham Hurlock and Elizabeth his wife, to William Gary - 100 acres, "Woodland Necke" formerly possessed by Daniel Walker - at the head of Woodenhawk Branch of King's Creek - adjoining land taken up by James Barber; and the land of John Edmondson and Joseph Sone. Wit: Wm. Hemsley, Charles Hemsley.

240 13 June 1689 Edward Stevenson, Planter, and Lettice his wife, to Richard Sweatnam, Carpenter - 200 acres called "Boadwell's" - adjoining land laid out for Thomas Wilkinson. Wit: Mic. Earle, Tho. Vaughn.

242 2 Feb. 1688 Robert Grundy, Gent. to Deborah Boydon, widdow, formerly ye relict of Thomas Impey, Gent., deceased. Deborah has 2 daughters, now living, by Thomas Impey, Sarah and Mary Impey. A marriage contract between Robert and Deborah - Robert agrees to allow Deborah to settle her estate, at her death or any time she shall deem fit; and one breeding mare at the day of marriage between Robert and Deborah. If Robert should have issue of Deborah then the plantation she now dwells upon called "Graves' Point" shall be given to such issue and for want of issue to Mary Impey and her heirs and for want of issue in Mary, then to Robert Grundy for life and then to pious uses of ye Catholick Church forever. Wit: Daniel Dunnavant, John Stanley.

243 20 Aug. 1689 William Gary and Grace his wife, to William Hemsley - 250 acres called "Old Mill" - taken up by James Scott, deceased and sold to Wm. Aldridge deceased, and lately settled on Grace Gary by the will of her father, George Aldridge, brother to the said William - on the east branch of Wye River adjoining land laid out for John Wright called "Knightley" - mentions Cabin Branch and adjoining land

laid out for Elizabeth Brewer. Wit: Thomas Emerson, William Scott, Thomas Anderson. Grace Gary examined privately before Edw. Man and Thomas Smithson.

244   20 Aug. 1689   William Hemsley, Planter, and Cornelya his wife, to William Gary_ - - - part of "Arcadia" at the head of Wye River on Williams' Branch - adjoining land taken up by Henry Collins and now in possession of Warner Sudall - land taken up by Henry Snowden called "Shore Ditch" - land taken up by Robert Noble called "Noble's Rainge" - land taken up by Richard Pedar - land taken up by Coll. Lloyd and Henry Costin called "Lloyd Costin" - containing 700 acres. Wit: Thos. Anderson, Thomas Emerson, William Scott.

245   3 Dec. 1687   William Scott and Soffiah his wife, to John Jones - "Triangle" in St. Michael's River, south side Bear Poynt Creek - adjoining John Wright's "Knightly" - mentions Cattaile Branch. Wit: George Craige, Robert Monday.

246   20 Aug. 1689   Robert Smith and Ann his wife, to James Wyatt - 300 acres called "Mantoon" in Talbot County on south side Chester River between land laid out for Richard Royston and a parcel formerly laid out for William Allen. Wit: Thomas Browne, Alice Glenvill.

247   1 Feb. 1688   Thomas Smithson, Gent., to John Preston, Planter - 100 acres on the west side of Bullingbrooke Creek called "Lydenburg" - adjoining Richard White and _____ Howes' land - beginning at an oak standing near the Great Road which leads from Peachblossom and the White Marsh to Howell Powell's plantation. Wit: James Smith, Robert Smith.

249   ____ 1688   Robert Smith, Gent. and Ann his wife, to Richard Mirax, Planter - 300 acres in the branches of Corsica Creek - part of "Wrexam Plaines," and part of "Smith's Forrest." Wit: William Coursey, William Hollinsworth.

249   1 Jan. 1689   Thomas Smithson, Gent., to Thomas Metcalfe, Planter - in consideration of one whole year's service already performed - "The Hazard" on a branch of Harris' Creek - adjoining land laid out for Henry Frith - 70 acres. Wit: John Llewellin, Samuel Withers. Smithson gave bond for 2800 lbs. of tobacco.

250   15 Jan. 1689   Christopher Baitson, Cooper, and Hannah his wife, to William Gwyen - 95 acres at the head of a branch of St. Michael's Creek, the plantation whereon C. Baitson lately dwelt - part of "Willingbrow" and part of "Bradford" - adjoining the land of James Scott. Mentions land laid out for (Henry) Frith. Wit: William Lawrance, Nicholas Lowe.

251   20 Jan. 1689   James Clayland, Clk., to Richard Sweatnam, Gent., 300 acres called "Bridgewater" - west side Unicorn Branch, Chester River - containing 300 acres - adjoining land of Thomas Smithson   Wit: James Downes, Francis Lathor, Elizabeth Davis.   Jas. Clayland to James Downes, P/A.

252 19 Nov. 1689 William Hemsley, Planter, and Cornelia his wife, to Nicholas Kelley, Planter - 100 acres, part of "Hemsley's Brittanica" at the head of Bread and Cheese Harbour Branch, Wye River - in the woods back of "Norminton" - adjoining Warner Sudall's "Lambeth" formerly laid out by Henry Costin. Wit: David Boyd, Thomas Crease, V. Hemsley.

252 20 Jan. 1689 Peter Peterson to Edward Smith - one-half of 400 acres called "Chesterfield" on Coursegall Creek, in Chester River, Talbot Co. boundaries according to patent. Wit: Robert Smith, Edward O'Dwyer.

253 18 Mar. 1689 Edward James of Kent County to John Winchester - 150 acres on Red Lyon Branch in Chester River, part of 1000 acres called "James' Camp." John Hawkins, Nicholas Hackett.

253 18 Mar. 1689 William Hemsley and Cornelia his wife, Planter, to John Payne and James Dolton, Planters - part of "Hemsley's Arcadia," 140 acres on Lobbs Creek - adjoining Rebecca Woolman; John Thrift and John Burd. Wit: Thomas Thomas, John Clemens.

254 18 Mar. 1689 John Aldridge to Thomas Bruff - moiety of 350 acres called "Indian Neck" on Wye River. Wit: Isaak Winchester, Phillip Hopkings, John Thrift.

255 19 Mar. 1689 Michael Hackett to Robert Smith - part of "Mt. Hope" and part of "Michael's Adventure" on Island Creek, Chester River - 250 acres according to patent. Wit: John Walker, Edward Pollard.

255 4 Mar. 1689/90 John Edmondson, John Pitt, John Wooters, William Stevens, Thomas Skillinton and William Dickinson to John Dickinson and John Boram - Arbitration of a piece of land between them.

256 1 June 1690 John Coppidge and Mary his wife of Kent Island, County of Kent, Gent., to Michael Miller of same county, Gent. - "Forrest Lodge" in Coursey's Creek, late the property of Disborow Bennett, of the Island, deceased - adjoining Macklin, 100 acres; also "Bennett's Addition," 150 acres adjoining - reference to the will of Disborow Bennett, dated 26 April 1676, devising "Forrest Lodge" to his wife, Mary. Wit: Phillip Corner, John Ellis. Mary Coppidge examined before William Lawrence and Samuel Wheeler, Justices for Kent County.

257 16 June 1690 Michaell Russell of St. Michael's River, Planter, to Benjamin Pride, Planter - one-half of "Fortune" on a branch of St. Michael's River - in the woods - adjoining Andrew Skinner - containing 150 acres. Wit: Thomas Williams, Thomas Bruff.

257 18 June 1690 William Vaughan of Dorset, Planter, and Mary his wife, to Alexander More of Talbot, Planter - one-half of two tracts formerly taken up between Vaughan and More - one called "Morefield," 94 acres and an additional tract adjoining, 30 acres. Wit: Wm. Hemsley, J. Downes.

258   14 June 1690   Zorababell Wells and Katharin his wife, Planter, to Samuel Withers - 100 acres, "Maiden Poynt Addition" on the south side St. Michael's River - adjoining "Maiden Poynt" laid out for Charles Hollingsworth. Wit: Henry Adcock, John Wrightson. Katharin Wells to John Power - P/A.

258   17 June 1690. Henry Woolchurch to his daughter Sarah, wife of James Berry - gift of love - 300 acres, part of "Mannour of Canterberry" on Tredhaven Creek, Choptank River. Wit: John Morrough, Lambert Clemens, John Lloyde.

258   18 June 1690   John Edmondson, Merchant, to Isaak Sassarson of Talbot, Planter - 300 acres called "The Playnes" - in Dorset County, south side Choptank River - adjoining Cuthbert Phelps - in Hunting Creek. Wit: James Murphey, Michael Earle.

260   24 July 1690   Peter Sayer of Wye River, Gent., administrator of Jonathon Sibery, late of Talbot, Gent., to James Smith, Gent. - "Wintersell"(?)- 200 acres on Coursegal Creek, Chester River - adjoining land of George Paskall. Wit: John Llondey, Samuel Smith.

261   19 June 1690   William Vaughan of Dorset County, Planter, to William Warner of Talbot, Planter - 15 acres, part of "Pooly's Discovery" at the head of Wye River between "Noble's Chance" and "Finney's Hermitage" - taken up by Wm. Vaughan and John Pooly. Wit: William Hemsley, Matthew Eareckson.

262   __ July 1689   John Miller, Planter, to John Fisher of Talbot - 100 acres called "Miller's Hope" at the head of Bullinbrooke Creek - adjoining "White Phillips." Sig: "Weltham Miller." Wit: J. Saywell, Joyce Habland.

262   18 Aug. 1690   Henry Pratt, Planter, and Seth his wife, to Thomas Yewell - 150 acres, the plantation and dwelling wherein Henry Pratt and Seth his wife now dwell - part of "Willton," formerly laid out for Thomas Williams at the head of Middle Branch, Wye River - adjoining Andrew Skinner's "The Triangle." Mentions John Morgan, Cabbin Cove, Richard Sweatnam, Edward Barracliffe. Wit: John Lamb, Thomas Collins, Nicholas Clouds.

263   19 Aug. 1690   Thomas Yeowell, Planter, to Henry Pratt, Planter - 200 acres at the head of Williams' Branch, Wye River, called "Lincoln." Wit: Thos. Collins, John Lamb, Nico. Clouds.

264   19 Aug. 1689   Sarah Yeowell, wife of Thomas, to Henry Pratt - release of her dower to above land. Wit: Thos. Collins, John Lamb, Nico. Clouds.

264   10 Aug. 1690   Robert Frampton, Planter, to John Robinson, Planter - 122 acres called "Frampton" west side of Tuckahoe, in the woods - west side of the land formerly laid out for John Wooters called "Dunmore Heath," "Moorefield," George Bowes; and "Coventry." Wit: John Price, J. Saywell.

265 16 Aug. 1690 James Smith and Margaret his wife, to James Willson -
100 acres, part of "Smith's Delight" on the south side of Chester River - adjoining James Willson's plantation and a parcel of land sold by
James Willson to William Bush, "Hamer's Addition." Wit: Richard Gold,
Elizabeth Pearle, William Ganum.

266 28 June 1690 John Mountford, Planter, of Thirdhaven Creek, administrator of Thomas Mountford, deceased, to John Edmondson, Merchant -
150 acres, part of "Tilghman's Fortune" - mentions land surveyed for
Samuel Tilghman - also with the plantation 5 cows, 2 calves, a 5 yr.
old steer, 2 yearling calves and 1 sheep. Wit: Edward Green, William
Rodeney.

266 John Mountford, Mariner, to John Offley - P/A. 28 June 1690.

267 15 July 1690 John Edmondson of Tredhaven, Mcht., to Joseph Rodgers -
part of "Tilghman's Fortune." Wit: Samuel Withers, Owen Jones.

267 19 Aug. 1690 Sarah Bishopp, executrix of Benjamin Hancocke, Ann Hancocke and Samuel Mott of Pensillvania by John Stanley, Attorney, to
John Edmondson - 100 acres at the mouth of Tredhaven Creek called "Westland." Wit: John Bishopp, John Brooke. Sarah Bishopp and Ann Hancocke
acknowledge a letter of Attorney before Justice of the Peace of Kent
County - Will. Berry, Clk. Witnesses John Bishopp, James Brooke.

265 Kent Co. Territory of Pennsilvania. Sarah Bishopp, executrix of the
will of Benjamin Hancocke of Talbot, deceased, to Samuel Mott of Kent
County - P/A. 5 da 12 mo called July, 1690. Sig: Ann Hancocke.

265 24 Feb. 1689/90 Samuel Mott of Kent Co., Territory of Pennsilvania to John Stanley -
transfer of his P/A. Wit: Owen Jones, Andrew Imburd.

267 18 Aug. 1690 Thomas Collins of Talbot, and Barbara his wife, to Geo.
Mallony of Talbot - 500 acres called "Killman's Plaine" on Unicorne
Branch, Chester River; the portion conveyed being 100 acres. Wit:
John Masters, John Offley.

269 8 Aug. 1690 Barbara Collins to Nicholas Clouds - P/A.

269 17 June 1689 Nicholas Clouds, Gent. and Nottley his wife, to Thomas
Bruff - 500 acres, "Nottlar's Enjoyment," on the northeast side of
Andrew's Branch, Chester River. Wit: Wm. Hemsley, William Clayton,
John Pitt, Thomas Collins.

270 18 Aug. 1690 Notlar Cloudes to Thomas Collins - P/A. Wit: Luke Heys,
Margaret Gouldsmith.

270 28 June 1690 John Switt, Marriner of London, to Richard Dudley - 200
acres called "Dudley's Demesne" - in the woods at the head of a branch
of Tuckahoe Creek adjoining "Dudley's Choice" and "Bugby." Wit: Thos.
Fisher, Thos. Allcocke. Acknowledged by Capt. John Switt, 18 June 1690
before George Robotham and William Finney.

271 16 Sept. 1690 Charles Hollingsworth to Robert Smith - 100 acres, called "Rocka Nooke" and 50 acres adjoining given by Robert Martin by his will unto Charles Hollingsworth, south side St. Michael's River, south side Rockanoke Creek. Wit: Anthony Lynch, Nicholas Hackett.

271 30 Mar. 1690 Vincent Lowe, Esq. to John Edmondson, Merchant - 1000 acres called "Stratton" on the fresh runs of Tuckahoe Creek. Wit: Chas. Robinson, Samuell Withers, John Hazelwood.

272 15 Sept. 1690 Abraham Morgan of Talbot, Planter, and Elizabeth his wife, to William Sharpe, Merchant - by virtue of the last will and testament of Emanuel Jenkinson, Merchant - "Upland" - patented 10 Aug. 1683 to Emanuel Jenkinson being the predecessor to Abraham Morgan - adjoining "Poplar Ridge" and "Addition"- containing 300 acres. Wit: Nicholas Lowe, Benjamin Hunt. Elizabeth Morgan examined privately before E. Man and John Stanley, Justices of the Peace.

273 10 Mar. 1689 John Stanley, Gent., and Judith his wife, to James Bishopp - 100 acres, one-half of 200 acres called "Chance" on a branch of Tredhaven Creek near Thomas Cox's land and the land of Thomas Hutchinson called "Hull." Wit: Edward Pollard, Luce Man, Fitz William Lawrence. Acknowledged by John and Judith Stanley 8 Sept. 1690 before Edw. Man and Thomas Powell.

274 20th day Nov. 1689 MEMO: On the back side of a conveyance of 300 acres made over by Robert Smith, Gent., to Richard Mirax, Planter. Robert Smith acknowledged the deed before John Llewellin, Clerk. Also, on 28 June 1690 Solomon Wright, Atty of Ann Smith, acknowledged the same deed before John Llewellin, Clerk.

274 19 Nov. 1690 Henry Pratt, Planter, and Seth his wife, to Richard Sweatnam, Gent. - in consideration of five pounds sterling, lawful money of England - convey 30 acres, part of "Willton" - laid out for Thomas Williams on Mill Branch, Wye River - adjoining Edward Barraclift and the land sold to John Morgan. Wit: James Downes, Anthony Rumball.

275 20 Nov. 1690 Henry Pratt and Seth his wife acknowledged the above in open court. J. Llewellin, Clerk.

275 19 Nov. 1690 John Thrift, Planter, and Mary, his wife, to John Pursell, Sr., Cooper, and Charles Neall, Planter - 100 acres, part of 220 acres purchased of William Hemsley, Gent., called "Hemsley's Arcadia" at the head of Wye River - adjoining Rebecca Woolman. Wit: James Downes, Anthony Rumball.

276 20 Nov. 1690 John Thrift and Mary his wife, acknowledged in open court. J. Llewellin, Clk.

276 17 Nov. 1690 Philemon Armstrong and Mary his wife, to Robert Gosse - 200 acres, "Armstrong's Marsh" - in the woods between the branches of St. Michael's River and King's Creek near "Londonderry." Wit: John Warner, John Jones, Peter Dod.

277 18 Nov. 1690 David Blaney, Planter, and Katherine his wife, to Thomas Thomas, Planter - 300 acres on the western side of Back Wye River - called "Woodstock." Wit: Wm. Coursey, Thomas Jackson.

278 20 Nov. 1690 David Blaney and Katherine, his wife, acknowledge the deed for 300 acres called "Woodstock." John Llewellin, Clk.

278 18 Mar. 1689 William Hemsley, Planter, and Cornelia, his wife, to Philemon Hemsley - 100 acres, "Hemsley's Brittania" - between the branches of Tuckahoe and Wye River - adjoining "Betts' Chance," "Norminton" and "Stevens Plaines." Wit: Frances Armstrong, John Dames.

279 20 Nov. 1690 Wm. Hemsley and Cornelia his wife acknowledge above deed. John Llewellin, Clk.

279 19 Nov. 1690 John Buly, Planter, to William Watts, Planter - 100 acres called "Stanfords' Poynt" - formerly taken up by Robert Evans, deceased, lately in the occupancy of Henry Pott (Pratt?) - given by Robert Evans to John Buly as a gift, in his will - near the mouth of St. Michael's Creek, Talbot Co. Wit: John Longe, Thomas Earle.

280 18 Oct. 1690 Thomas Mettcalfe, Planter, to Francis Porter - 70 acres called "The Hazzard" on a branch of Harris Creek, adjoining land laid out for Henry Frith - on the main road and a path called Clay's Path, being rough, uncultivated land. Wit: Hugh Sherwood, Henry Adcocke.

280 18 Nov. 1690 Francis Armstrong, Planter, and Lettice his wife, to Wm. Hemsley, Planter - L45 sterling and 100,000 pounds of tobacco - 4000 acres called "Cranberry Forrest" in Cecil County, on the Pennsilvania Road - at the dividing of the road at the going over of Back Creeke - the one to the head of Elk River, the other to the towne of Newcastle. Mentions land taken up by Capt. Henry Warde called "Loungacre." Also "The Leavell" in Cecil County south side of Sassefras River - adjoining George Williams' Neck, on the upper side of Chester River, 1500 acres, Wit: William Harris, John Dames.

281 20 Nov. 1690 Francis Armstrong and Lettice his wife acknowledged in open court. John Llewellin, Clk.

281 10 Nov. 1690 John Paine and Martha his wife and James Dalton to Ralph Jackson, Merchant - 140 acres, 140 acres, part of "Arcadia" surveyed for William Hemsley. Wit: Wm. Hatfield, Wm. Hemsley, John Pooly.

282 15 Nov. 1696 Francis Shipard and Elinor his wife, to John Primrose - 100 acres, south side Chester River, north side Jones' Creek - part of "Shipard's Fortune," laid out for Francis Shipard. Wit: Robert Draughton, Richard Skinner, John King.

283 15 Nov. 1690 Francis Shipard to John Primrose - Bond. Wit: R. Draughton, John Morryde.

283 24 Mar. 1689 Mary Mayle, executrix of Anthony Mayle, to Robert Smith -

in consideration of Ł170 sterling money of Old England - 100 acres -
"Cabbin Necke" and "Goose Necke," 100 acres in Tredhaven - also a plantation in St. Michael's River,   part of a tract laid out for Roger Grosse
and conveyed by William Grosse to Anthony Mayle, 250 acres. Wit: Alexander Cunningham, Michael Earle.

284   24 Mar. 1689 Mary Mayle acknowledged before James Smith and William
      Finney.

284   16 Oct. 1690 Robert Smith, Gent., and Ann his wife, to Robert Gouldes-
      borough, Gent. - 250 acres of land conveyed 18 Nov. 1864 by William
      Gross and Hester his wife, to Anthony Mayle - on St. Michael's River,
      part of 800 acres surveyed for Roger Gross, Gent., called "Ashby."
      14 Oct. 1689 Anthony Mayle willed to Mary, his wife. Wit: Robert Hawk-
      shaw, Nicholas Clouds, Daniel Swindell.

285   20 Nov. 1690 Acknowledged by Robert Smith and Ann his wife, by Nich-
      olas Clouds, Atty..

285   12 Jan. 1690 John Dickenson of Talbot, Planter, to James Bampton,
      Blacksmith - 100 acres called "Hoggsdon" on the upper side of Evans'
      Bay, Choptank River. Wit: John Stanley, Thomas Bowdle, Robert Gouldes-
      borough. Acknowledged 8 Jan. 1690 by John Dickenson before Edward Man,
      John Stanley and Thomas Bowdell.

286   14 Feb. 1684 John Harwood of Talbot, Carpenter, to John Dine, Planter -
      part of "Rich Farm" and "Rich Farm Addition," on the fresh runs of
      King's Creek - adjoining Robert Harwood's "Rich Farm;" the land of
      John Pitt formerly taken up by the Chancellor - containing 200 acres.
      Wit: Samuel Smith, Edmond Webb. Acknowledged before Vincent Lowe.

287   12 Jan. 1690 William Porter to David Farebank - 100 acres, "Belfast"
      in the Second Branch of Second Creek - adjoining "Camper's Neck;" land
      laid out for Thomas Camper, and "Fairlee." Wit: John Wrightson, John
      Meires.

288   17 Mar. 1690/1 William Porter by his Attorney, James Sedgwick, acknow-
      ledged the above. John Llewellin, Clk.

288   14 Mar. 1690 Alexander Mecotter, Planter, from Mary Jenkinson, wife
      of Robert Jenkinson, late of Talbot, Planter - refers to a letter of
      Attorney written 12 June 1688 by R. Jenkinson to Mary Jenkinson - em-
      powering her to sell his lands - Mary sells to A. Mecotter part of
      "Sutton Grange," where the said Mary lately dwelt - west side Bulling-
      brooke Creek, lately conveyed to her as Mary Mecotter, widow, by the
      said Alexander Mecotter. Wit: Solomon Wright, Robert Gouldesborough.

289   17 Mar. 1690/91 Mary Jenkinson in behalf of her husband, Robert Jenk-
      inson, acknowledges the deed. John Llewellin, Clerk.

      15 July 1689 Robert Jenkinson of Talbot, Planter, to wife Mary Jenkin-
      son, P/A. Wit: George Cowley, John Swallow, John Viner.

289   13 Mar. 1690 Thomas Collins, Jr. to Thomas Hindes - 100 acres, "Spread
      Eagle" on the southeast branch of Chester River, adjoining Thomas Sea-
      ward. Wit: Lucke Heyes, Honer Gorashan(?)

290   16 Mar. 1690 George Phillips, Talbot, Planter, and Mary his wife, to
      Claudius Dutitre,, Taylor - 80 acres called "Spring Branch" - adjoining
      "Forlorn Hope." Wit: Wm. Gisson, John Goodyan(?)

      17 Mar. 1690 George Phillips and Mary his wife by her attorney, Richard
      Bishopp, acknowledge. John Llewellin, Clerk.

290   1 Dec. 1690 Thomas Smithson, Gent., to John Lydingham, Planter - 230
      acres, part of "Micklemire" - on Galloway Branch, King's Creek - adjoin-
      ing part sold to John Wright and "O'Maly's Range." All rough, unculti-
      vated land. Wit: Michell Turbutt, Elizabeth Marlingbourn.

291   17 June 1690 William Hemsley, Planter, and Cornelia his wife, to Jo-
      seph Vickars, Planter - 200 acres, part of "Padding Towne" at the head of
      Brewer's Branch, Wye River - adjoining "Dunn's Range," taken up by John
      Dunn and a part sold to William Hadden. Wit: Rich. Royston, Michell
      Earle.

292   10 Mar. 1690 William Watts, Planter, to Edward Floyd, Planter - 30 acres
      on St. Michael's Creek - adjoining "Nominie" and the land of Solomon
      Thomas - part of "Nominie." Wit: Thos. Delehay, Thomas Hughes.

293   10 Mar. 1690 William Watts, Planter, to Thomas Hughes, Planter - 100
      acres called "Stampford" - near the mouth of St. Michael's Creek - paten-
      ted to Robert Evans, deceased, and willed to John Buly and by John Buly
      to Watts. Wit: Tho. Delehay, Edward Floyd.

294   16 June 1691 Robert Smith, Merchant, to Walter Riddell, Tanner - 100
      acres, "Lampton" on Elliott's Branch, Chester River - adjoining land laid
      out for Robert Smith lately in possession of Daniel Demsley(?) - also
      "Smith's Range." Wit: William Finney, William Hemsley.

295   14 Aug. 1690 Robert Smith and Ann his wife, to George Phillips, Plan-
      ter - 250 acres adjoining the land of George Powell. Wit: Daniel Swin-
      dell, Christopher Spry, Charles Weebb.

296   16 Mar. 1690 Joseph Rogers, Planter, and Mary his wife, to Erick Im-
      britson of Talbot, Planter - 20 acres, part of "Westland" - laid out for
      John Edmondson, now occupied by Erick Imbartson - on Fox Creek adjoining
      the land called "Ashford" possessed by Rogers and William Harris and the
      remaining land of William Ridgway. Wit: Jeffrey Hardman, Mary Bennitt.

297   20 Sept. 1690 Mary Jenkins to Edward Vering, Planter - part of "Sutton
      Grange" on the north side Choptank River, western branch of Bullenbrooke
      Creek - adjoining Richard White's part of "Sutton Grange." Wit: Edward
      Lydenham, Joseph Attkins. Mary Jenkins acknowledges before Edward Man
      and John Stanley, two of his Lordship's Justices.

297 17 Mar. 1690 Charles Ferris, Carpenter, to William Finney, Tanner - 300 acres at the head of Frenchwoman's Branch, Tuckahoe Creek, part of the land called "Dances'." Wit: Thomas Smithson, Robt. Gouldesborough.

298 1 May 1691 Charles Ferris acknowledges before Edward Man and Richard Carter, Justices.

298 17 June 1691 John Browne of Wye River, Planter, and Elizabeth his wife, to Richard Carter of St. Michael's River, Merchant - in consideration of thirty five pounds sterling (£35) and 10,000 lbs. of tobacco - part of the land laid out for Thomas Williams called "The Addition" - on Williams' Branch, Back Wye River - lately purchased of Henry Pratt by Wm. Young. Part of "Partnership," 350 acres adjoining, lately purchased of William Young - together with one dwelling house, plantation and clear ground. Wit: Thomas Smithson, J. Standley.

299 17 June 1691 John Browne acknowledged before George Robotham and John Standley.

300 22 June 1691 James Downes, Gent., to Richard Sweatnam, Innholder - 320 acres called "Hopton" (except 20 acres laid out for the county's use and reserved for that purpose in his patent, dated 20 Dec. 1681) - on the east side of the eastern branch of Back Wye - adjoining James Scott's "Old Mill" and the land of Richard Woolman. Wit: James Sedgwick, John Llewellin.

301 22 June 1690 James Downes acknowledged before Edward Man and James Smith, Justices.

301 30 June 1691 John Standley, Gent., and Judith his wife, to John Swallow, Taylor - 139 acres called "Timber Neck Addition" - on Miles Creek - in the woods - adjoining "Taylor's Ridge." Wit: Fitz William Lawrence, Thomas Delehay.

302 30 June 1691 John Stanley to John Swallow - Bond. Wit: Fitz William Lawrence, Thomas Delehay, John Whittington.

302 8 June 1691 James Ross of Wye River, Chirurgion, to Richard Carter of St. Michael's River, Merchant - 300 acres, part of "Finney's Hermitage" - purchased from Joseph Sampell late of St. Mary's, which Joseph Sampell had by deed of gift from William Finney and heretofore possessed by William Watkins late of Talbot County - on a branch of Wye River and a part of the same tract possessed by Moses Harris. Wit: Thomas Smithson, Thomas Besswicke. Delivered 13 Aug. 1691 and witnessed by Smithson, Besswicke and Samuel Withers.

303 8 June 1691 James Ross to Thomas Smithson, P/A. Wit: Thomas Besswicke, Margaret Nash. Acknowledged before George Robotham and Wm. Finney.

303 17 Jan. 1690 John Edmondson, Merchant, and Sarah his wife, to William Dixon - in consideration of 500 acres known to be William Ridgway's land in Little Duck Creek, Territory of Pensilvania - a moiety or half

of "Stratton" - 1000 acres on the fresh runs of Tuckahoe Creek - to be
equally divided between them. Wit: Richard Noble, William Barton. Ack-
lowledged by John Stanley, Attorney. John Llewellin, Clerk.

304 22 Dec. 1690 John Edmondson and Sarah his wife to Samuel Millson -
1000 acres - one-half of "Stratton" on the fresh runs of Tuckahoe Creek.
Wit: William Jones, Richard Garratt. Acknowledged by John Stanley, Atty.

19 Jan. 1690 Sarah Edmondson to John Stanley - P/A.

305 20 Jan. 1690 John Hambleton of Talbot to John Primrose - 150 acres in
Talbot on the south side of Chester River, north side of Dividing Branch -
adjoining "Price's Hill" on Hambleton's Creek - my part, the lowermost,
of "Hambleton's Hermitage." Wit: Richard Bishope, Phill. Hemsley, Samuel
Taylor.

306 11 Dec. 1690 John Paddison, Planter, and Elizabeth his wife, to Francis
Harrison, Planter - 100 acres of land given to Paddison and William Rich
by the last will and testament of William Rich, deceased - part of "Taylor's Ridge" at the head of St. Michael's Creek running into Great Choptank River. Wit: John Arrington, Thomas Anderson.

307 11 Dec. 1690 Elizabeth, wife of John Paddison, examined privately for
her consent before Thomas Fisher and John Stanley, Justices.

308 20 Nov. 1690 James Bampton, Blacksmith, and Elizabeth his wife, to Joshua Atkins - 100 acres called "Chance" - on the east side of Island Creek -
first taken up by Edward Roe and sold to Thomas Games, Sr. and by Games
to Bampton - adjoining the land of Francis Parrott formerly laid out for
Andrew Skinner - and the land of Robert Curtis. Wit: John Swallow, Joseph Bell.

308 20 Nov. 1690 Elizabeth Bampton examined privately before Edward Man and
Thomas Bowdell.

308 16 Aug. 1691 Robert Smith, Gent., and Ann his wife, to Edward Clarke of
Talbot, Shewmaker - 400 acres of land in Tuckahoe Creek called "Parker's
Farme" - adjoining "Dudley's" and the land of Thomas Hammond and John Jad-
win. Wit: John Davis, Jacob Gibson.

309 3 Aug. 1691 John Lewis of Talbot, executor of the last will and testament of Walter Bouncell of Talbot, deceased, to Robert Smith - 100 acres,
part of a parcel formerly laid out for John Boge, deceased, known as
"Bougley" - on Corsica Creek. Wit: Charles Weeb, Nicholas Clouds.

310 16 Aug. 1691 John Lewis from Robert Smith - 100 acres called "Plaines" -
in Chester River, Winchester Creek - mentions a road to William Hinson's -
John Chairs' land and the land of John Smith. Wit: C. Weeb, Nic. Clouds.

310 15 Aug. 1691 John Hawkins, Gent., and Judith his wife, to William Bolton,
Planter - 200 acres, part of "Tully's Delight" - southeast branch of Ches-
ter River. William Coursey, Attorney for Judith Hawkins. Wit: William
Godwin, William Sparkes.

312 15 Aug. 1691 William Bolton, Planter, and Sarah his wife, to John Hawkins, Gent. - the plantation whereon the said William Bolton now liveth -
175 acres on Dividing Creek, south side Chester River - part of "Macklinborough," formerly belonging to Mary Hawden. Wit: William Godwin, William Sparks. William Coursey, Attorney for Sarah Bolton.

313 15 Aug. 1691 Sarah Bolton to William Coursey - P/A.

313 18 Aug. 1691 Thomas Wallis, Shoemaker, to Robert Smith, Gent. - 100
acres called "Neglect" - north side St. Michael's River near the land of
Francis Maudling called "Batchelor's Branch" - according to certificate
dated 27 May 1681. Wit: Fitz William Lawrence, John Robins.

314 10 Aug. 1691 Robert Smith, Attorney to Walter Lester, to John Harwood
of Dorset - 200 acres called "The Freshes" - on Miles Creek - adjoining
James Scott's land called "New Mill" - Gouldesborough's land and Taylor's land. Wit: Samuel Withers, Nicholas Clouds.

314 2 Aug. 1691 John Harwood of Dorset, to Elizabeth Underwood and Judith
Underwood, daughters and co-heirs of Peter Underwood late of Dorchester,
deceased - in consideration of 50 acres (one-half) in Dorchester Co.
called "Castle Haven" sold by Elizabeth and Judith Underwood to him -
conveys 100 acres called "The Freshes" near St. Michael's Creek in Talbot County. Wit: Joseph James, Richard Moore, Symon Cuper.

315 16 June 1691 John Pursell, Cooper, and Mary his wife, to Andrew Fallon,
Merchant - 200 acres on Williams' Branch, Wye River, adjoining "Willton."
Wit: Solomon Wright, David Deane, James Saywell.

315 20 Jan. 1691 John Johnson, only heir of the deceased Albert Johnson,
and his mother-in-law Alice Greene, wife of Henry Greene, to William
Pell - 100 acres called "Hope" - on Hambleton's Creek, Chester River -
granted to Albert Johnson, patent issued 2 May 1683. Wit: John Hawkins,
William Cowell, Richard Hazeldine.

316 11 Aug. 1691 Rouland Hambridge of Talbot, Millwright, to William Moore,
Planter - 100 acres called "Buckbey" or "Buckley" - in a fork of a branch
on the west side of Tuckahoe Creek, back of "Smith's Clifts" - mentions
a division tree between Hambridge and Henry Ayler - now in possession of
William Moore. Wit: Jonas Davis, Jacob Bradbury, Nicholas Lowe.

317 10 Nov. 1690 John Lane, Planter, and Mary his wife, to Thomas Anderson,
Chyrurgion - 300 acres, my part of "Lane's Forrest" - in the woods between Tuckahoe Creek and the eastern branch of Great Choptank River -
adjoining "Wolverton," formerly laid out for William Kirkham and Clement
Sayles' land called "Edmondson's Green Close." Wit: John Wittington,
Thomas Allcocke, Francis Vickars. Acknowledged by John and Mary Lane be-
for Edward Man and Richard Carter.

318 9 July 1691 Daniell Jenifer of Accomack Co., Va., to Thomas Allcocke of
Talbot - 500 acres called "Advantage" on the sorth side of Great Chop-
tank River adjoining land formerly laid out for Ralph Williams called
"Beaver Neck" - mentions Beaver Neck Creek. Wit: George Johnson, George

Cay, Daniel Thomas Jenifer. Acknowledged by Coll. George Robotham, Attorney, before Edward Man and Richard Carter. John Llewellin, Clerk.

319 Accomac. 9 July 1691 Daniel Jenifer before John Wallop, Justice of The Peace, County of Accomac, acknowledged the above deed. Daniel Jenifer to Coll. George Robotham of Talbot County - P/A. Wit: George Johnson.

20 Feb. 1692/3 Thomas Smithson to Thomas Allcocke - Receipt for ten shillings - alienation fee.

319 14 Sept. 1691 Robert Worters and Elizabeth his wife, to John Heatherington - 50 acres, part of "Smith's _____ " - formerly taken up for Robert Smith on north side Wye River - on Morgan's Creek - mentions Long Neck. Wit: Vinc. Hemsley, Luck Atcheson, Attorney for Elizabeth Worters.

320 19 Sept. 1691 Elizabeth Worters to Luck Atcheson - P/A.

320 14 Sept. 1691 George Hurlock, Planter, and Elizabeth his wife, to John Hawkins, Gent. - 200 acres called "Brampton" - south side Chester River in Talbot County - adjoining land laid out for George Read. Wit: Thos. Smithson, Sarah Bridges, Joane Vaughan.

321 14 Sept. 1691 Elizabeth Hurlock to Thomas Smithson - P/A. Wit: Edward Elliott, Jane Vaughan.

321 11 Aug. 1691 Thomas Camper to David Fairbanke - 100 acres, "Camper's Neck" - on the north side of the second branch of Second Creek on Camper's Cove. Mary, wife of Thomas Camper gives her consent. Wit: John Power, Thomas Mason.

322. 11 Aug. 1691 Mary Camper to James Sedgwick - P/A. Wit: Thomas Mason, Dennis White.

322 18 Aug. 1691 Thomas Smithson, Gent., to Benjamin Pride - 100 acres, "Brafferton" on Mill Branch, St. Michael's River - taken up by Smithson. Adjoins Carter's store and land called "Winckles' Fortune." Wit: Richard Macklin, John Llondey.

323 19 Aug. 1690 Cornelius Mullraine, Planter, to Francis Chaplin - Bond - refers to a deed dated 16 June 1684 to Francis Chaplin for 500 acres, "Broad Oake" now in his tenure. Wit: Joseph Wiggott, Thomas Logens, Dennis Connolly.

323 16 June 1691 Jacob Hooker and Benjamin Hooker, sonns of Thomas Hooker late of Ann Arrundell County, deceased, to Job Evans, Merchant, of Ann Arrundell - refs. to a patent issued to John Edmondson, Mcht., 2 July 1668 for 600 acres called "Wallnut Ridge" in the woods at the head of the western branch of Choptank River - on 10 May 1673 Edmondson conveyed to Thomas Hooker who willed it to his sonns Jacob and Benjamin. Wit: Peter Sayer, John Edmondson. Acknowledged before George Robotham and John Davis.

325 19 Oct. 1691 George Blades and Frances his wife, to Edward Elliott - 50 acres called "Harley" - south side St. Michaell's River adjoining the land laid out for John Hollingsworth. Wit: Benjamin Pecke, James Auld.

325 10 Oct. 1691 Robert Betts to Oliver Millington - 100 acres, "Betts' Chance" - in the branches of Tuckahoe Creek in the woods - adjoining the land sold by Robert Betts to Robert Johnson and Daniel Baker. Wit: Anthony Rumball, Elizabeth Sweatnam. Acknowledged in open court. J. Llewellin, Clerk.

326 10 Oct. 1691 Robert Betts to Oliver Millington - 100 acres near the head of a branch of Tuckahoe Creek, called "Betts' Addition" - adjoining "Betts' Chance" and the land called "Epsom." Wit: A. Rumball, Elizabeth Sweatnam.

326 22 July 1691 Robert Smith, Gent., and Ann his wife, to Samuel Withers - 250 acres in Island Creek, Chester River - part of "Mt. Hope" and "Hill's Adventure" 250 acres according to patent. Wit: Jonathon Dickkins, Susana Hubbard, William Alderne.

Ann Smith to Nicholas Clouds - P/A. Wit: Daniel Glover, Solomon Wright.

327 20 Oct. 1690 William Hemsley, Gent., and Cornelia his wife, to Richard Sweatnam - 230 acres, part of 348 acres called "Hemsley's Farme" - metes and bounds according to patent granted to W. Hemsley, 26 Feb. 1688. Wit: Vincent Lowe, Nicholas Lowe.

328 20 Oct. 1691 Robert Smith and Ann his wife, to William Sparkes - 200 acres on Island Creek, Chester River, known as "Wright's Choice." Thomas Beckles, Solomon Wright.

329 18 Oct. 1691 Robert Smith and Ann his wife, to Jeofrey Mattershaw - "Jamaica," 100 acres south side Chester River near the branches of Corsica Creek and "Jamaica's Addition" adjoining "Danby" - formerly laid out for Richard Jones, 50 acres. Wit: Richard Hinson, Nicholas Clouds, Susana Hubbard, Francis Vickars.

330 19 Oct. 1691 William Hemsley to Charles Hollingsworth - 300 acres, part of "Jerusalem" being 400 acres - formerly laid out for John Hollins - and ye 300 acres lately alienated to William Hemsley by John Hollins - on the south side of Chester River in Talbot County. Wit: Nicholas Lowe, John Hawkins.

331 12 Oct. 1691 Thomas Bevan and Pretitia his wife, executrix of the will of William Ramsey late of Anarundel County, deceased, to John Jurdan - in accordance with the will of Wm. Ramsey, written 12 May 1689, sells 300 acres called "Sintra" on Coursegall Creek, Chester River in Talbot. Wit: John Turnley, Christopher Spry, Matthew Smith.

12 Oct. 1691 Acknowledged by Robert Smith, Attorney for Thomas and Pretitia Bevan. John Llewellin, Clerk. John Jurdan to Nicholas Clouds - P/A. 12 Oct. 1691.

331 20 Oct. 1691 William Hemsley, Gent., to Richard Sweatnam - 118 acres, part of "Hemsley's Farm" - the remainder of a tract of 330 acres. Wit: Vincent Lowe, Nicholas Lowe.

332 21 Oct. 1691 Richard Woolman of Talbot, Gent., to Thomas Bruff, Innholder - all of a tract of land called "Addition" at the head of the southeast branch of St. Michall's River - adjoining a plantation laid out for Richard Woolman, Sr., deceased - also a parcel of 200 acres, adjoining. Wit: Wm. Hemsley, John Edmondson, Christopher Denny.

332 21 Oct. 1691 Robert Smith to William Godwin - 100 acres on south side Chester River, north side of Elliott's Branch, a branch of Island Creek- part of "Wright's Choice" formerly laid out for Nathaniel Wright. Wit: Solomon Wright, Thomas Beckles.

334 22 May 1689 Jeoffrey Mattershaw of Talbot, Planter, to Richard Sweatnam, Carpenter - 100 acres, "Paxton's Lott" at the head of the branches of Back Wye River - adjoining "Butterfield" - land laid out for Matthew Mason and Harbert Craft - and land called "Green Spring." Wit: Robert Smith, Kympt. Mabbett, Thomas Delehay.

334 17 Oct. 1691 William Tonge, Gent., executor of John Robertson late of Talbot, deceased, to Robert Smith - (Robertson's will written 20 March 1689)- 150 acres on the southwest branch of Coursegall Creek called the Muddy Branch - 150 acres, "Jamaeka" and "Jamaeka Addition." Wit: Francis Vickars, Nicholas Clouds.

335 17 Oct. 1691 Robert Smith, Gent., and Ann his wife, to George Smith - 200 acres, part of "Smith Farme" - adjoining "Salisbury" and "Provident." Wit: John Johnson, Rachel Hinson, Susana Hubbard.

336 17 Oct. 1691 Nathaniell Wright to Robert Smith - 300 acres according to patent, called "Wright's Choice" - on the southeast branch of Island Creek in Chester River. Wit: Thomas Beckells, Solomon Wright.

336 21 Oct. 1691 William Sparkes and Mary his wife, to Samuel Withers - 200 acres on the north side of Island Creek, Chester River, called "Sparkes' his Owne" - and 100 acres called "Sparkes' Choice" - adjoining "Mt. Hope" and land laid out for John Michell. Wit: Solomon Wright, John Salter, John Chase, Jr.

338 13 Jan. 1690 Robert Smith, Gent., and Ann his wife, to Edward Baning - "Goose Neck" - 50 acres on north side Choptank River, on the western side of Plaindealing Creek running out of Threadhaven Creek. Wit: Thomas Moore, Edward Russam.

338 5th day, 4th month called June, 1690 - Benjamin Parratt, Planter, to John Jadwin - one-half of "Parratt's Lott" - adjoining John Jadwin's own land. Wit: Henry Adcock, Jacob Abrahams.

339 12 May 1691 Lovelace Gorsuch of Talbot to William Sharpe, Merchant -

"The Wilderness" on the north side of Choptank River on ye Long Point -
adjoining the land of Clore Odore, Planter, bought of Edward Lloyd, and
the land of Thomas Martin - containing 600 acres. Wit: Samuel Martin,
William Jones, Josiah Boush.

Acknowledged 21 July 1691 by Lovelace Gorsuch before Edward Man and.
Thomas Bowdle.

339   30 June 1691 John Stanley, Gent., and Judith his wife, to John Swallow,
Taylor - 139 acres called "Timber Neck Addition" on a branch of Miles
Creek, back in ye woods - adjoining "Timber Neck" and "Taylor's Ridge."
Wit: Fitz William Lawrence, Thomas Delehay.

Acknowledged by John and Judith Stanley, 6 July 1691 before Edward Man
and William Bexley.

340   3 June 1691 John Stanley to John Swallow - Bond. Wit: Fitz William
Lawrence, Thomas Delehay, John Whittinton.

340   17 Nov. 1691 Edward Hambleton, Planter, to Richard Feddeman, Taylor -
100 acres, part of "Price's Hill" on south side Chester River, on a
branch called the Southeast Branch - adjoining part of "Price's Hill"
which belongs to Samuel Hambleton. Wit: Daniel Sherwood, Thomas Hopkins, Jr.

341   24 Mar. 1691/2 James Downes to Richard Sweatnam - Bond. Wit: John
Llewellin, James Sedgwick, John Valliant.

342   15 9ber 1691 John Bennett of Ann Arundale County and Sarah Bennett als
Homewood, his wife - legatee, relict and executrix of John Homewood,
late of Ann Arrundale County, Gent., deceased, to Richard Purnell -
reference to a patent issued 17 May 1666 to Andrew Skinner, a parcel
of land called "Rich Range" on the west side of the northwest branch
of Choptank River - adjoining land laid out for John Homewood for 500
acres.   On 20 July 1672 Skinner sold to John Pawson and he, 2 August
1677 bequeathed to John Homewood, all his land in Maryland, about 1700
acres, and John Homewood soon after dyed, and as by his will written 2 August 1681 bequeathed to his beloved wife Sarah Bennett alias Homewood,
the plantation whereon he dwelt for her natural life, called "Homewood's
Lott," by survey 1,010 acres; also to Sarah his wife, a tract in Patap-
sco River, 400 acres near Bodkin Point called "Homewood's Rainge,"
during her natural life and by reversion of the two parcels to his kinsman Thomas Homewood, sonn of his brother Thomas Homewood, deceased, and
further John Homewood bequeathed to Sarah Bennett alias Homewood, all
land, housing and plantations he had in his possession or revertion, to
him belonging in Maryland except the aforesaid 2 parcels mentioned -
she to make over to Coll. William Colebourne of Sumersett County, 150
acres adjoining ye said Colebourn's land out of ye tract called "Holme
Hill" at Tuckahoe in Talbot County and made Sarah sole executor. And
after his death Sarah entered into the 500 acres of which she and John
Bennett convey one-half (250 acres) of "Rich Range" to Richard Purnell.
Wit: Thomas Austin, Edward Wilkinson. Acknowledged by John Pitts in
open court by virtue of a letter of Attorney.

343 15 Xber 1691 John Bennitt and Sarah Bennett his wife, to John Pitts -
Power of Attorney. Wit: Thomas Austin, Edward Wilkinson.

343 11 Dec. 1690 John Paddison of Talbot, Planter, and Elizabeth his wife,
to Francis Harrison, Planter - a parcel of land formerly granted to J.
Paddison and William Riche, both of Talbot, by the will of William
Riche, deceased - 100 acres, part of "Taylor's Ridge" at the head of
St. Michaell's Creek. Wit: John Anderson, Thomas Anderson.

11 Dec. 1690 Elizabeth Paddison examined before Thomas Fisher and John
Stanley.

Other Heritage Books by R. Bernice Leonard

Queen Anne's County, Maryland Land Records, Book 1: 1701–1725

Queen Anne's County, Maryland Land Records, Book 2: 1725–1741

Queen Anne's County, Maryland Land Records, Book 3: 1738–1747

Queen Anne's County, Maryland Land Records, Book 4: 1743–1755

Talbot County, Maryland Land Records, Book 1: 1662–1675

Talbot County, Maryland Land Records, Book 2: 1676–1691

Talbot County, Maryland Land Records, Book 3: 1692–1702

Talbot County, Maryland Land Records, Book 4: 1702–1712

Talbot County, Maryland Land Records, Book 5: 1712–1725

Talbot County, Maryland Land Records, Book 6: 1725–1733

Talbot County, Maryland Land Records, Book 7: 1733–1740

Talbot County, Maryland Land Records, Book 8: 1740–1745

Talbot County, Maryland Land Records, Book 9: 1745–1751

Talbot County, Maryland Land Records, Book 10: 1751–1758

Talbot County, Maryland Land Records, Book 11: 1758–1765

Talbot County, Maryland Land Records, Book 12: 1765–1771

Talbot County, Maryland Land Records, Book 13: 1771–1777

Talbot County, Maryland Land Records, Book 14: 1777–1784

Talbot County, Maryland Land Records, Book 15: 1784–1790

www.ingramcontent.com/pod-product-compliance
Lightning Source LLC
LaVergne TN
LVHW021521080426
835509LV00018B/2601